Meaningful Assessment in Interdisciplinary Education

Meaningful Assessment in Interdisciplinary Education

a practical handbook for university teachers

Ilja Boor

Debby Gerritsen

Linda de Greef

Jessica Rodermans

First published in 2021 by Amsterdam University Press Ltd.

Published 2025 by Routledge
4 Park Square, Milton Park, Abingdon, Oxon OX14 4RN
605 Third Avenue, New York, NY 10158

Routledge is an imprint of the Taylor & Francis Group, an informa business

© I. Boor, D. Gerritsen, L. de Greef, J. Rodermans / Taylor & Francis Group 2021

All rights reserved. No part of this book may be reprinted or reproduced or utilised in any form or by any electronic, mechanical, or other means, now known or hereafter invented, including photocopying and recording, or in any information storage or retrieval system, without permission in writing from the publishers.

Trademark notice: Product or corporate names may be trademarks or registered trademarks, and are used only for identification and explanation without intent to infringe.

ISBN: 9789463729048 (pbk)
ISBN: 9781003699477 (ebk)
NUR 143

Volume 7 of the Series Perspectives on Interdisciplinarity
Cover design : Matterhorn Amsterdam

DOI: 10.5117/9789463729048

Every effort has been made to obtain permission to use all copyrighted illustrations reproduced in this book. Nonetheless, whosoever believes to have rights to this material is advised to contact the publisher.

For Product Safety Concerns and Information please contact our EU representative: GPSR@taylorandfrancis.com
Taylor & Francis Verlag GmbH, Kaufingerstraße 24, 80331 München, Germany

Contents

	Acknowledgments	8
	Introduction	9
	Why this handbook?	9
	Structure of this handbook	10
Part 1	**Getting started with the assessment of interdisciplinarity**	**12**
	Meaningful assessment	13
	Assessing with the right purpose in mind	14
	Providing powerful feedback	18
	Making use of authentic assessment	20
	Aligning the assessment with learning outcomes	23
	Aligning the asssessment with pedagogical beliefs and values	24
	Assessing the skills that foster interdisciplinarity	25
	Definitions: multidisciplinary, interdisciplinary, and transdisciplinary	25
	Subskills and learning outcomes	26
	Assessing integration	27
	Assessing critical thinking	28
	Assessing collaboration	29
	Assessing reflection	31
Part 2	**The examples**	**34**
	How to navigate the examples	35

1	Assessing perspective-taking skills with a simulation game	37
2	Making 'big ideas' tangible with an installation	42
3	Self-assessment of boundary-crossing competences	47
4	Peer feedback on the reflection of a stakeholder dialogue	54
5	Experiencing the learning process using a portfolio	58
6	A rubric for interdisciplinary capstone projects	64
7	Making failure a learning tool for collaboration skills	71
8	Evaluation of the golden principles of collaboration	77
9	Reflection on teamwork and disciplinary expert roles	82
10	A moot court to build critical thinking skills	86
11	Authentic assessment, learning by accident	90
12	Grading the contributions to class discussions	94
13	Dance assessment as experiential learning	98
14	Enhancing critical thinking with Perusall	103
15	Co-creation of a rubric to encourage ownership of learning	107
16	Peer and self-assessment for student-led activities	113
17	From feed-up to feed-forward	120
18	Comparative judgment as a tool for learning	125
19	The co-creation of assessment criteria	129
20	Reflection on interdisciplinary competences using a portfolio	135

Final remarks: towards new ways of assessment — 141
    Lessons learned for meaningful assessment in interdisciplinary education — 141
    Taking the next steps — 143

Index — 145

References — 150

Colophon — 153
    About the authors — 153
    About the series — 153
    About the University of Amsterdam — 154
    About the Institute for Interdisciplinary Studies — 154
    Contact — 154

Acknowledgments

When is assessment meaningful? How can we give university teachers useful tools to develop their courses and evaluate whether or not students are making progress in acquiring the skills that are needed for interdisciplinarity? As program managers and senior lecturers of interdisciplinary programs, we were confronted with these questions ourselves and wanted not only to describe how this assessment could be designed but above all to show concrete examples. It took time to find the right focus, and it has been our quest to find the examples that show how to get started in the context of university teaching. We are therefore very grateful for all the enthusiastic cooperation and input we received from lecturers and staff at the University of Amsterdam as well as other universities within and outside the Netherlands. We are thankful that so many lecturers who have been pioneers in meaningful assessment of interdisciplinary skills have been willing to share their experiences in this handbook. Without them, this handbook would not have been possible.

We would like to thank all the lecturers who have contributed their examples to this handbook: Jorien Zevenberg, Anco Lankreijer, Joost Krijnen, Dora Achourioti, Karen Fortuin, Judith Gulikers, Carla Oonk, Nanke Verloo, Marjoleine Boersma, Coyan Tromp, Eric Mazur, Wendy Nuis, Mien Segers, Kostas Nizamis, Maarten Blom, Hein de Haas, Lela Mosemghvdlishvili, Erwin van Vliet, Frank Cornelissen, Mieke Lopes Cardozo, Sandra Cornelisse, Michiel Schuurman, Alena Anishchanka, Jennifer Thewissen, Pascal Wilhelm, Jose A. Alvarez Chavez, and Merel van Goch. We also would like to acknowledge all other colleagues and students who helped shed extra light on the examples: Luca Eijgenraam, Inge van der Welle, Tom Lentz, Lucy Wenting, Roosmarijn van Woerden, Iwan Oostrom, Femke Bokma, Mary Herboldt-Soudant, Yorike Hartman, Julia Sassi, Ida Kemp, Hilde Creten, Machiel Keestra, Julie T. Klein, and Lina Dokter.

Introduction

Why this handbook?

Our world faces major societal challenges – population growth, climate change, the availability of quality freshwater, waste reduction, large human migrations, the faster spread of viruses – that require the next generation of graduates to be able to make a difference. These challenges are complex because they involve interactions across components that are unpredictable and because they are often accompanied by a high degree of uncertainty. Universities are expected to play a critical role both in conducting research and in educating a new generation of academic professionals who are committed to the public good and capable of responding to the challenges of an uncertain world. Calls for a strong connection between academia and the rest of society are growing. Science, technology, and innovation are seen as the breeding ground for the societal and economic innovation that is necessary for the well-being of society. Backward mapping these perspectives to courses and degrees shows an increasing need and interest for interdisciplinary and transdisciplinary education. Academic institutions that successfully harness the potential of interdisciplinary research and education while keeping the right balance between disciplinarity and interdisciplinarity will be able to reap major benefits, positioned as they will be at the center of a system that produces knowledge to improve the lives of many (Wernli, Darbellay & Maes, 2016). It is no wonder, then, that the number of student projects, courses, and degrees with an interdisciplinary approach has been growing and that assessing this kind of education has become an increasingly pressing question. How can we meaningfully assess interdisciplinary learning?

We are faced with the challenge of educating our students to see beyond the limits of their own discipline and to come up with innovative, integrated solutions to our contemporary challenges. Many lecturers have started to rethink the education they are offering and are helping to initiate change. We see university teachers who, besides transferring knowledge, want to put more emphasis on teaching students how to integrate knowledge, to collaborate, to think critically, and to reflect. We know lecturers who are breaking down the barriers not just between scientific disciplines but also between academia and society, allowing different types of knowledge to play a role in academia. They are responding to the changing role of universities in society and the changing needs of a new generation of professionals.

Just as teaching and learning are ready for change, so is assessment. A lecturer is faced with the challenge of assessing students daily. But to assess more complex or higher-order skills-oriented learning outcomes that are common in interdisciplinary projects and courses is quite a challenge.

This handbook is of interest to you if you are looking to be inspired to implement innovative assessment methods that assess higher-order skills and/or interdisciplinary learning outcomes rather than assessing solely the acquisition of knowledge. If you and your team are looking for ways to assess integration, collaboration, reflection, and critical thinking, the examples in this handbook point to new directions in assessment and provide illustrations of inspiring initiatives.

To sum up, interdisciplinarity is on the rise in higher education, but we are still at the onset of systematically answering the question of how to meaningfully assess interdisciplinary learning outcomes. With this handbook, we want to give this a kick-start by explaining interdisciplinary understanding and presenting ample examples of pioneers who are showing us how to introduce the necessary changes to make our education future-proof. We hope that this handbook will give you a foothold for initiating changes in your assessment practice.

Structure of this handbook

The book is divided into three parts. In the first part – *Getting started with the assessment of interdisciplinarity* – we explain why we think that meaningful assessment drives student learning and how feedback is a crucial element in learning. We also provide an overview of what interdisciplinary understanding is, including the necessary skills and knowledge that constitute interdisciplinary understanding and frequently used learning outcomes.

The second part of the book includes examples of assessment methods used in practice. The examples vary across a range of academic disciplines and institutional settings. Some examples are taken from interdisciplinary courses; others are used within a more disciplinary context. However, all examples can be applied to courses and student projects with interdisciplinary learning outcomes or can be adapted in such a way that they can be applied within your course, regardless of the discipline from which the course stems.

The examples in this handbook show methods to assess not only student work such as integrative final papers, student portfolios, and capstone presentations but also the outcome of simulation games, the learning process of students, and the way students collaborate. The examples explain how the change to meaningful assessment was implemented. There is a focus on what innovation in assessment comprises as well as on the assessment methods themselves, with helpful formats, rubrics, and reflection questions. Our intention is to provide a representative variety of inspiring good practices that cover the most important aspects of interdisciplinary understanding.

Education has changed dramatically as a result of the COVID-19 pandemic, with the distinctive rise of distance learning whereby teaching is undertaken remotely and on digital platforms. We acknowledge that this situation may require other assessment methods to be used. Some of the examples are suitable for online assessment; for others, a digital alternative may be able to be developed.

In the third and final part of this book – Towards new ways of assessment – we summarize the lessons learned and good practices found from the examples in this book. We also outline the steps that can be taken to get started.

The reason we wrote this handbook is straightforward: we want to share good practices of interdisciplinary skills assessment that are already used in higher education, including our classrooms. By doing so, this book will hopefully serve as a foothold for designing and implementing innovative assessment methods for projects and courses. Both lecturers and educational developers can take the examples given in this book and adjust them to fit their own situation, regardless of whether they are working on an interdisciplinary course or a course that focuses more on one discipline.

Part 1
Getting started with the assessment of interdisciplinarity

In part 1, we explain why we think that meaningful assessment drives student learning. In this chapter, we will elaborate on the theories and foundations of meaningful assessment in interdisciplinary education. We also provide an overview of what interdisciplinary understanding is, including the necessary skills and knowledge that constitute interdisciplinary understanding and frequently used learning outcomes. The information in this chapter is meant to give you a foothold for starting to change your assessment practice.

Meaningful assessment

Society today needs more than passive graduates who have complied with a standardized assessment regime. It requires academics who can direct and reflect on their own learning process and development. When searching for examples for this handbook, our starting point was that if we want to educate a new generation of academics who can take charge of what they learn, how they learn, and how they grow, it is essential for assessment to maximally strengthen learning.

The development of curricula with higher-order learning outcomes such as integration, critical thinking, collaboration, and reflection requires new ways of thinking about assessment that go beyond assessing the lower-level learning outcomes of reproduction and the application of knowledge.

The responsibility of educating a new generation and the corresponding new developments in curricula made us realize that new ways of assessing are required and that meaningful assessment is the best fit.

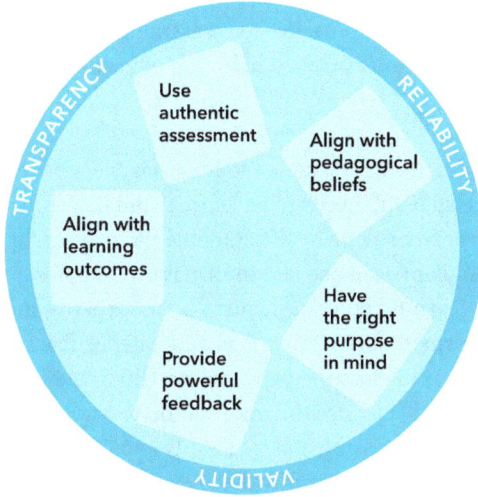

Figure 1: Building blocks for meaningful assessment in interdisciplinary education

We argue that there are five building blocks that can contribute to the meaningfulness of assessment:
1 assessing with the right purpose in mind;
2 providing powerful feedback;
3 making use of authentic assessment;
4 aligning the assessment with learning outcomes;
5 aligning the assessment with pedagogical beliefs and values.

Below, we elaborate on these foundations and explain why they are necessary for meaningful assessment in interdisciplinary education.

Assessing with the right purpose in mind

Earl and Katz (2006) state that if assessment is designed for the right purpose, it has enormous potential to strengthen students' learning. They argue that all assessments should be considered feedback. The examples in this handbook focus on how to reach strengthening students' learning by using three different purposes – assessment *of* learning, assessment *for* learning, and assessment *as* learning. These three types of assessment serve a valuable but separate purpose.

Assessment of learning

Assessment *of* learning is summative and evaluates the quality of students' learning based on criteria by assigning a mark value to represent that quality. It usually takes place at the end of a course and is used to determine the extent to which a student has achieved the intended learning outcomes. Summative assessment can have far-reaching consequences for students because it determines whether or not they have passed a course. Therefore, lecturers have a responsibility to use the appropriate assessment method to make accurate, consistent, and fair statements about the competence of their students. In the next chapter of this handbook, we provide many examples of innovative approaches to assessment based upon assessment *of* learning because this is a common practice in higher education.

Assessment for learning

Assessment *for* learning is designed to make visible what each student already knows and can do and what still needs to be learned and therefore must be incorporated in the course. This can be done by the students themselves, by their peers, and/or by the lecturers. Students can use this information to monitor their progress toward achieving their learning outcomes and to be more active in their learning. Thus, the purpose of assessment *for* learning is to generate feedback on learning and to inform students about how to close the gap between where they are and where they aim to be. Lecturers, in turn, can use the information to find out where their students are and how they are progressing and to identify gaps or misconceptions. Thus, it can also be used by lecturers to identify the specific learning needs of students, to provide feedback to students, and to get feedback on their teaching strategies in order to adjust them accordingly. There is no rule about what formative assessment should look like. In essence, any activity that provides students or lecturers with information about the learning process can be used as assessment *for* learning – for example, self-evaluation with a rubric, peer feedback on an essay, or a quiz in a lecture. Quite a few examples of innovative approaches to assessment we provide in the next chapter are based upon assessment *for* learning. In several cases, the assessment innovations are motivated by a desire to make student assessment a better and more educational experience for students.

Assessment as learning

Assessment *as* learning is more about reflecting on the learning process than about the learning process itself, since it emphasizes assessment as a metacognitive process. This type of assessment stimulates students to constantly seek and receive constructive feedback and to reflect on their own learning process with the aim of achieving deeper understanding. Therefore, this assessment type focuses on explicitly stimulating the ability of students to become independent, critical self-assessors (Earl and Katz, 2006). Assessment *as* learning stems from the idea that learning is an active process of cognitive restructuring that takes place when students deal with new information. In order to do so, students must develop an ability to monitor the quality of their own work. This capacity, in turn, requires that students have the evaluation skills to objectively compare the quality of their own work in relation to high-quality work and that they can modify their own work accordingly. It might seem that the role of the lecturer is diminished in the assessment *as* learning, since it revolves around students. However, the role of the lecturer is still important and shifts to designing structured assessment *as* learning opportunities that allow students to think about and monitor their own learning and adjust it accordingly (Earl and Katz, 2006). In this handbook, you can find examples of assessment *as* learning where students develop their own grading rubric (example 15 and 19) and put together a portfolio (example 5).

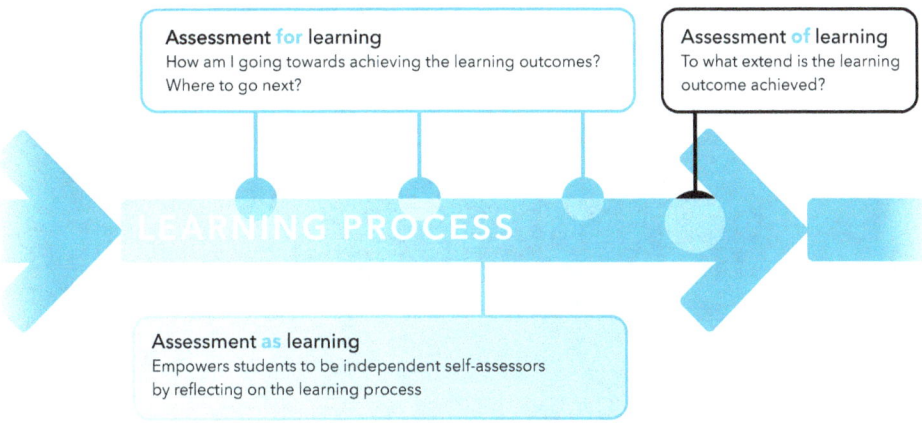

Figure 2: The purpose of assessment: assessment for, as, and of learning

Assessment procedures and methods can and should contribute to student learning in addition to measuring it. We must acknowledge that student learning across the higher education curriculum is complex and multifaceted and may need to be assessed in a wide variety of ways. Our stance is to recognize that all types of assessment *of*, *for*, and *as* learning can be meaningful when it is purposefully used.

Case study: Assessment with the right purpose in mind, BA and BSc in Engineering, Harvard University

The learning outcomes of the course *Applied Physics 50* are to provide students with insights into how science applies to the real world and to teach students skills such as self-directed learning that will be useful in their future careers. The lecturer, Eric Mazur, developed an assessment system for this semester-long freshman course that combines the different purposes of assessment *of*, *for*, and *as* learning. The students' work is assessed using an innovative approach called specification classification (based on Nilson & Stanny, 2014). The system contains three major components.

The first component is that there are clearly defined assignment specifications that are closely related to the intended learning outcomes (constructive alignment). At the start of the course, students are given a clear description of what is considered to be a satisfactory completion of the assignment.

The second component is that students receive a lot of feedback during the course (assessment *for* learning). Students only receive a final grade at the end of the semester (assessment *of* learning), after they have handed in several assignments in each category (for example, project presentations and reports). The grade at the end of the semester depends on the number of assignments that have met the specifications. If an assignment does not yet meet the specifications, students have additional opportunities to show that they can meet the standards. This means that the final grade reflects what the students have accomplished by the end of the semester and not simply what they accomplish during a specific assignment. The advantage of this approach is that it relieves students of the pressure of high-stakes exams because they are given a lot of room to make mistakes without negatively affecting their final grade. Furthermore, they receive timely feedback that guides them in how they can improve their learning. The aim of this assessment system is for students to focus on their learning process and to improve their self-directed learning skills (assessment *as* learning).

The last component is the flexibility of the assessment system. Students determine when they do activities and when and how they are assessed. One way to achieve this is for students to hand in a virtual 'token' to submit revised work to meet the specifications, to upgrade their grade, or to postpone the deadline for an assignment by a week. This component also contributes to assessment as learning.

All work submitted by students is evaluated on the so-called EMRN scale (see figure 3) that gives students more nuanced feedback on their performance than a binary system (i.e. pass or fail). An E (E= exceptional) or an M (M= meets expectations) mean that the work of the student meets the expectations set for that specific assignment, while an R (R=revision required) or an N (N=not assessable) mean that the work does not yet meet the specifications. Then the final grade is determined by the number of assignments for which the student has met the specifications.

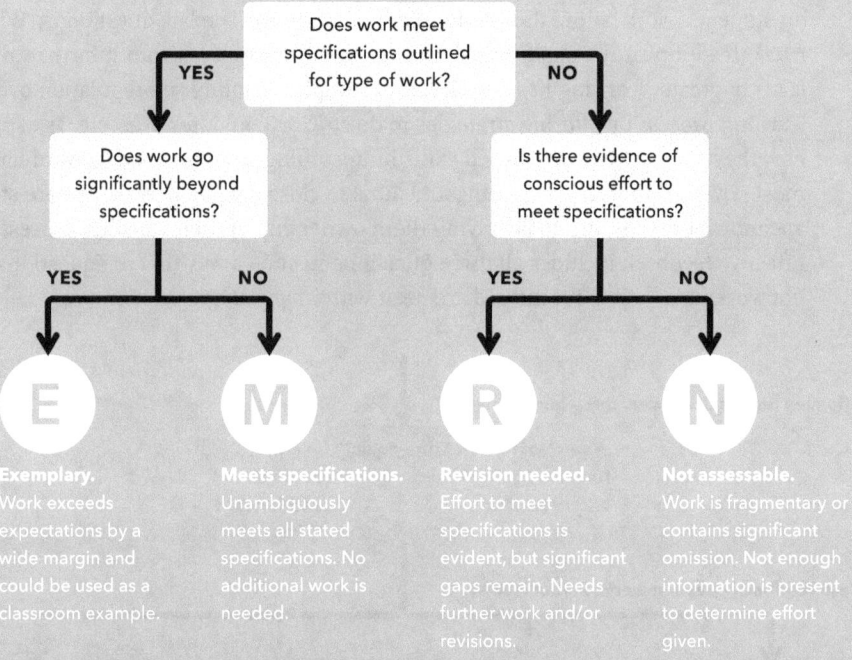

Figure 3:   Schematic representation of the EMRN scale

In this course, Mazur wants to create a culture that encourages creativity and calculated risk-taking – one that takes the stigma out of failure. He designed the activities and assessment system so that they leave ample room for student errors without compromising their eventual success or final grade.

Providing powerful feedback

Earl and Katz (2006) argue that all assessments should be viewed as feedback because it informs students about their learning process. According to Hattie and Timperley (2007), the main purpose of feedback is to reduce the gap between students' current understanding of the subject matter and their intended learning outcomes. Deciding on the purpose of assessment guides you as a university teacher on how to give effective and powerful feedback to students. The question is when and how feedback is powerful in different forms and purposes of assessment.

Hattie and Timperley define three different questions that need to be answered for effective feedback. The first question is: *Where am I going?* (feed-up). Feed-up is essentially about understanding the learning objectives, the criteria for success, and what high-quality work looks like. For example, providing a rubric with assessment criteria is considered feeding up. The second question they distinguish is: *How am I going?* (feedback). Feedback is information about the students' progress in meeting an expected standard (for example, comments by peers or lecturers, or self-evaluation on students' work before they hand in a final version). The last question is: *Where to next?* (feed forward). Feed forward means providing students with information that leads to greater learning possibilities, for example, enabling self-regulation over the learning process by offering strategies to do so. You could, for example, ask students how they can improve on learned skills in upcoming courses. Feed forward has the most powerful impact on learning and aims to close the gap between where students are and where they aim to be, giving them ownership of their learning process. Effective feedback includes all three questions in such a way that the questions do not work in isolation but instead are dealt with in an integrated manner.

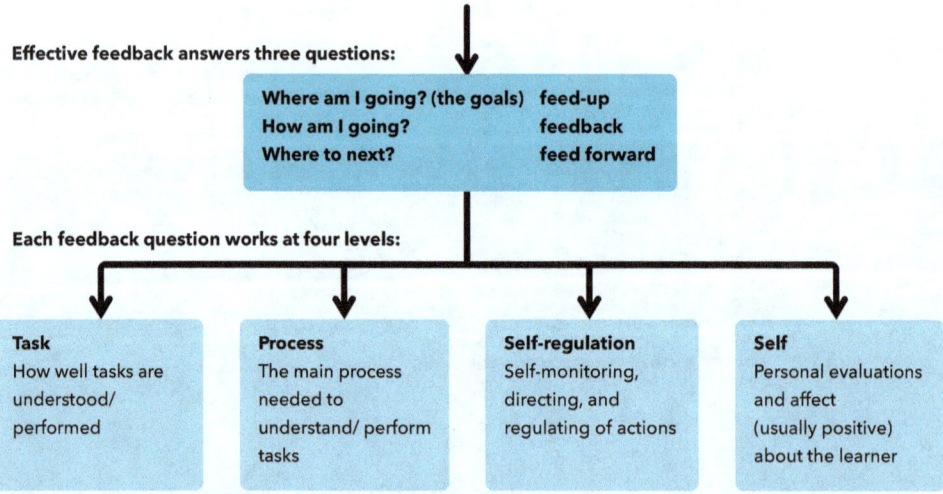

Figure 4: Hattie and Timperley's feedback model (2007)

Feedback works at four different levels: task, process, self-regulation, and the self. The three questions of feedback (feed-up, feedback, and feed forward) can be asked at any of these levels. Feedback on the task level concerns information about how well the task is performed. Feedback on the task level is often called corrective feedback and is very effective because it provides students with targeted information on their performance when working on a task. Feedback on the process level deals with the underlying processes of the task, such as the way in which students detect their own mistakes or in which order they come to a solution. Feedback at this process level teaches students how they learn and can also be applied to other tasks or assignments. On the self-regulation level, students develop internal and cognitive feedback mechanisms that allow them to monitor, direct, and regulate actions toward the learning objectives. Feedback at this level enables students to monitor their own progress and act accordingly to meet the intended learning outcomes. Through this feedback, students learn to learn more independently. Feedback on the last level – the self-level (usually praise) – is considered the least effective feedback and can even be counterproductive since it offers limited information on how students can develop themselves. In general, feedback is considered effective on the levels of process and self-regulation. The different levels of feedback are interrelated, although feedback is most powerful if it proceeds from the task to the processing of the task to self-regulation that continues beyond the task (Hattie and Timperley, 2007). The more information the feedback contains, the more effective it is. High-information feedback includes information on the different feedback levels and shows students not only their mistakes but also why they made these mistakes and what they can do to avoid making the same mistakes again (Wisniewski, Zierer & Hattie, 2020).

For feedback to be effective, it is important to keep a few things in mind. Feed-up, feedback, and feed forward should be offered at the right moment in the feedback cycle and at the right level (task, process, or self-regulation). Feedback is a dialogue rather than one-way communication. For example, you could ask the student 'What do you need?' or 'What do you think?'. This enables students to take control of their own assessment by making them active participants in the process. Feedback will be more effective when a student is receptive to it because students who seek feedback tend to use this feedback. Furthermore, there are some basic conditions that should be kept in mind such as being specific and clear in your feedback, making sure students interpret the feedback in the right way, aligning with the students' level of understanding, and offering a safe learning environment when giving feedback to students.

> **Case study: Feed-up, feedback, and feed forward at the self-regulating level, Integration practicum, BSc in Interdisciplinary Social Sciences, University of Amsterdam**
>
> *Integration practicum* is a first-year course of the bachelor's program in Interdisciplinary Social Sciences at the University of Amsterdam in which students work for four weeks on a transdisciplinary research project in small groups of three to four students. The practicum has a different theme every year, for example human trafficking, and inclusion and exclusion. Two intended learning outcomes of this course are:
>
> 1. problem-solving skills (the analysis of a societal problem by including multiple perspectives and developing relevant and feasible solutions to this problem);
> 2. cooperation skills (working in small groups and recognizing the strengths and unique contributions of team members in order to formulate solutions to the problem).
>
> Part of the practicum is a self-reflection on the obtained skills during the course. Students formulate their personal learning objectives concerning problem-solving and cooperation skills at the beginning of the course (feed-up). Examples of personal learning objectives include learning to integrate theories from previous disciplinary courses and the integration of academic and professional knowledge. During the course, assessment *as learning* is applied by having students monitor their own progress (feedback). After every meeting, students reflect on how they worked on their personal goals by keeping a personal log. Writing personal reflection reports can be quite difficult for students at first. Therefore, students need to learn how to reflect on their own progress, and it is recommended that they include self-reflection as an academic skill in their program. By the end of the integration practicum, students are able to formulate a new personal learning objective based on a self-assessment. This personal learning objective can provide input for upcoming integration practicals in the bachelor's program of Interdisciplinary Social Sciences.

The importance of feedback in assessment will be visible in Part Two of this handbook. Many best practices integrate the 'feed-up, feedback, feed forward' cycle and apply the appropriate levels (task, process, and self-regulation) of feedback.

Making use of authentic assessment

Our contemporary society needs university graduates who are critical thinkers, who have the ability to collaborate in diverse teams, and who reflect on their actions. The Organisation for Economic Co-operation and Development (OECD) emphasizes the increasing importance of skills for professionals such as problem-solving, metacognition, creativity, collaboration, and analytical thinking as well as social and emotional skills such as empathy, persistence, and the ability to maintain focus on long-term goals (OECD, 2014). A report by McKinsey articulates the importance of personal and professional skills in the job market of the future: 'More work activities will require social and emotional skills and advanced cognitive capabilities, such as high-level logical reasoning capabilities that are required today for only a relatively limited number of jobs. This will be a challenge for education, training, and skill assessment models, which for now do not always emphasize "soft skills" such as social and emotional reasoning and sensing.' (McKinsey Global Institute, 2017). The development of so-called transferable skills that are useful for professional life requires an authentic learning approach in which learning activities take place in – or resemble – a real-life context for students. The assessment of authentic learning is concerned with more complexities because the goal in authentic learning is the acquisition of higher-order thinking processes and competencies instead of factual knowledge and basic skills (Gulikers, Bastiaens & Kirschner, 2004).

Authentic assessment is defined by Gulikers, Bastiaens, and Kirschner (2004) as 'an assessment requiring students to use the same competencies, or combinations of knowledge, skills, and attitudes, that they need to apply in the criterion situation in professional life'. They describe five dimensions of authentic assessment. First, the *task* should be authentic, which means that the students are confronted with activities that are common in professional practice. For a task to be authentic, students should perceive the task as representative, relevant, and meaningful for professional practice. The *physical context* is the second dimension of authentic assessment, and it represents how close the assessment context imitates reality. In addition to the physical context, the *social context* affects the authenticity of assessment. This dimension claims the importance of including in the assessment social processes – for example, collaboration – that represent the social context in reality. The fourth dimension is the *assessment result* or *form*. An authentic assessment result or form consists of a quality product or performance that students have to produce in real life. Furthermore, the assessment result demonstrates that students possess the competencies needed to achieve this result. In authentic learning, it is not likely that students are able to demonstrate in one test all the skills and competencies needed to perform an authentic task. Therefore, different assessment methods should be combined to cover the assessment of professional behavior. Additionally, students should present their work to others to defend their work and to demonstrate that they have mastered the authentic task that is being assessed. The last dimension is *standards and criteria*. In authentic learning, it is important to make standards and criteria explicit and transparent because this guides learning, just as in professional life, where individuals are usually evaluated on known criteria. Also, standards and criteria should represent relevant professional competencies and should resemble criteria used in real-life professional situations.

We argue that authenticity of assessment can contribute to the meaningfulness of the assessment. Authentic assessment gives students the opportunity to learn in a real-world setting. It gives lecturers the space to evaluate and provide feedback on the professional development of students. Therefore, assessment *for* and *as* learning—as discussed earlier in this chapter—should be attuned to authentic contexts. Furthermore, authentic assessment corresponds with the goals of interdisciplinary education because it can be used to evaluate the acquisition of higher-order thinking processes and competencies. Another reason why authentic assessment is a foundation for meaningful assessment is that in authentic assessment, students are aware of the relevance of their learning activities and assessment for their future professional life, which in turn enhances their intrinsic motivation for learning.

Case study: Authentic assessment, minor Tesla, University of Amsterdam

Tesla is a semester-long program for students in the Faculty of Science of the University of Amsterdam who are in the final stage of their master's program. In addition to the application of their scientific knowledge and skills, the aim of the program is to improve students' skills in a number of areas: teamwork, dealing with complex problems, communication with stakeholders, project management, entrepreneurship, and self-reflection. To achieve this, students participate in a wide variety of training sessions, workshops, and assignments, but most of the time is spent on a project for a client. Students work for five months in small project groups (two to three people) on a complex challenge together with a company or societal organization. The challenges are in the field of technical innovations that can have a positive impact on society (e.g. sustainability or health innovations). In this way, students can integrate the knowledge gained in the classroom with their experiences in the project. The project requires students to work through complex issues, negotiate team dynamics, and interact with a diverse group of stakeholders. Students often work on location at the client. The project provides an authentic learning environment and challenges students in a way that goes beyond those provided by even the best case studies. For example, students contributed to the design of an aesthetic and energy-autonomous greenhouse for urban environments. They provided the client with an overview of state-of-the-art technologies for different greenhouse components, identified suitable crops for such a greenhouse, and provided a business model to successfully introduce what they dubbed the 'Power Plant' into the market.

Not all the competencies needed to execute the project successfully are assessed separately, and no grades are given during the execution of the project. But there is plenty of room for feedback: every Monday morning and

Friday afternoon, the project groups receive feedback from their lecturers and fellow students on their progress. As a conclusion to the project, students present the results to the client in a format that is applicable within the setting of the client. Students are encouraged to reflect on how the format relates to their client's project. For example, they can choose to develop a prototype, make a short documentary, or give a workshop for the client. In this way, the assessment resembles the activities and products that the students must be able to deliver after graduation. In addition, students write a report for their academic advisers. Two assessment criteria of the report are whether students identified and presented the necessary steps for a follow-up of the project (focusing on actual implementation by the client) and whether they conducted an impact analysis of the proposed innovation.

Student comments demonstrate the authentic nature of the program. For example, one student remarked: 'Tesla is very different from other academic experiences, as it gives me more room to experiment with things. In other courses, papers always need to be written in a very specific way, but in Tesla there is more room to try things in different ways and see how it works out.' Another student stated: 'You can learn so much more during the five months of project work than a regular 10-month academic year.'

Aligning the assessment with learning outcomes

Constructive alignment between learning outcomes, learning activities, and assessment criteria is essential for students to achieve their learning goals and to acquire deep learning (Biggs, 2011). The challenge in assessing interdisciplinary student work is to turn complex learning goals into concrete, observable, and thus assessable outcomes.

For the purpose of developing clear, intended learning outcomes, you could base your intended learning outcomes on the learning taxonomy of Bloom (1956). This learning taxonomy can give you the vocabulary to clearly express what level of achievement you expect from students. Many learning outcomes of interdisciplinary and transdisciplinary courses are located higher up in Bloom's taxonomy. The levels **synthesis** and **evaluation** appear quite often in interdisciplinary education. This holds true at both the bachelor's and the master's levels. Synthesis may be defined as the ability of students to put together different parts – i.e. methods, theories, and results across different fields and disciplines – and to create new patterns or structures or to propose alternative solutions or a more comprehensive result. Action verbs used to assess synthesis include: create, develop, modify, rearrange, revise, relate, and combine. Evaluation may be defined as the ability of students to judge, check, and critique the value of material for a given purpose. Much-used action verbs that assess evaluation include: assess, critique, convince, contrast, interpret, justify, and validate.

Aligning the asssessment with pedagogical beliefs and values

As stated in the last paragraph, alignment between learning outcomes and assessment methods is essential. When developing a course and deciding on an assessment strategy, it is also helpful to take into account your – often implicit – pedagogical beliefs or didactic values. Everyone operates on the basis of such beliefs. It can be detected in the grading policy as stated in the course syllabus, the role of the teacher in the classroom, or the implicit values that you want to impart to students. In addition to being present at the course level, these beliefs can exist at the program or even institutional levels. For example, Maastricht University offers problem-based learning, in which the learning principles of constructive education, learning in a relevant context, collective learning, and self-directed education are incorporated into all its education.

There is no simple recipe for effective didactic methods for teaching interdisciplinary understanding or the development of higher-order skills. But there are some approaches that appear to be particularly important for interdisciplinary learning and teaching such as coaching for teaching and learning, collaborative or problem-based learning, and team teaching (De Greef et al., 2017). For example, collaborative learning is an educational approach to teaching and learning that involves groups of learners working together to solve a problem, complete a task, or create a product. If you have a course in which students from various disciplines are enrolled and you want them to learn from – and develop their ability to work with – people from different backgrounds, it is imperative that you develop an assessment method that does justice to this didactic principle and learning outcome. Think of a group assignment in which the students together deliver an integrated piece in addition to their own disciplinary contributions.

If you aim to make your assessment more meaningful, it is important to assess students in a way that matches the didactic methods and pedagogical beliefs of your course or the program as a whole. Especially since these methods and believes greatly contributes to the learning climate of the course, study program or institute or university.

Assessing the skills that foster interdisciplinarity

The challenge for all of us is to seek ways to intertwine teaching and assessment in such a way as to maximize student learning. Now that we have discussed the foundations of meaningful assessment, we will introduce the skills and learning outcomes that foster interdisciplinarity.

The term interdisciplinarity has become a buzzword in higher education and has been used to describe varying types of education. In the following paragraphs, we will give a definition of interdisciplinarity and explain how it relates to other terms that are sometimes used interchangeably, such as transdisciplinarity and multidisciplinarity. We elaborate on underlying skills such as integration, critical thinking, collaboration, and reflection.

Definitions: multidisciplinary, interdisciplinary, and transdisciplinary

In their research on interdisciplinary work, Boix Mansilla, Miller, and Gardner (2000) present a definition informed by literature review, empirical research, and hands-on experience with lecturers and students. They define interdisciplinary understanding as the capacity by which individuals and groups integrate knowledge and modes of thinking drawn from two or more disciplines to produce a cognitive advancement – such as explaining a phenomenon, solving a problem, or creating a product – in ways that would have been impossible or unlikely through single disciplinary means. Interdisciplinary learners integrate information, data, techniques, tools, perspectives, concepts, and/or theories from two or more disciplines to craft products, explain phenomena, or solve problems (Boix Mansilla 2010). Other definitions include Klein and Newell's connotation (1996) of a process that may answer a question, solve a problem, or address a topic that is too broad or complex to be dealt with adequately by a single discipline or profession by drawing on disciplinary perspectives and integrating their insights through construction of a more comprehensive perspective.

The distinction between multidisciplinarity and interdisciplinarity relates to the way in which the integration of knowledge is achieved. With multidisciplinary thinking, disciplinary knowledge is analyzed, summarized, and presented without the attempt to integrate the knowledge. Multidisciplinary knowledge lacks the hallmark characteristic of interdisciplinarity, namely the integration of knowledge.

Today's challenges require integration not only between academic disciplines but also between multiple forms of expertise, both academic and non-academic. They require a transdisciplinary approach. For example, the field of health care could evolve into a knowledge-producing field that includes academics from a range of disciplines as well as stakeholders such as health care practitioners, patients, administrators, and policymakers who stand on equal footing and participate equally in the knowledge-creation enterprise. Transdisciplinary courses can go beyond all disciplines and involve intense interaction between academics and practitioners in order to promote a mutual learning process between them. The coproduction of knowledge with stakeholders in society with the aim of solving complex problems that originate in society is an obvious characteristic of these projects and courses. For example, a student may research how competing claims on land, water, fish, forest resources, and pollution/emission rights are negotiated and resolved at multiple levels of governance by different participants and how this impacts the well-being of the wider population.

Subskills and learning outcomes

According to De Greef et al. (2017), interdisciplinary understanding consists of a set of interrelated constituent subskills, knowledge structures, and attitudinal aspects that enable the synthesis of disciplinary insights and the construction of a more comprehensive perspective.

Figure 5: Skills and subskills that foster integration

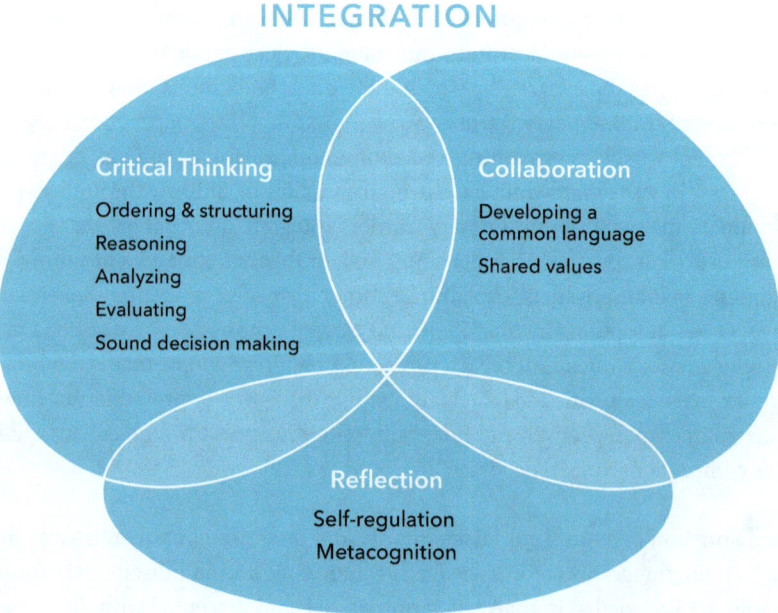

They distinguished the following constituent skills for interdisciplinary understanding: critical thinking, collaboration, and reflection. In this distinction, reflection is considered an essential supporting skill that is required for both critical thinking and collaboration. Integration is in this viewpoint an umbrella skill that can only be reached when the other skills are in place. The challenge in assessing interdisciplinary student work is to create concrete, observable, and thus assessable criteria.

Assessing integration

The ability to integrate different perspectives and multiple disciplines is an essential outcome of interdisciplinary and transdisciplinary projects, courses, and programs. This outcome means that students must be able to select relevant fields or schools of thought and can integrate information, data, techniques, tools, perspectives, concepts, and/or theories into a relevant whole in order to solve a problem, develop a product, or explain a phenomenon. Although integration is key to interdisciplinarity and transdisciplinarity, this can involve many different ingredients. Klein (2010) states that no universal theory or model of integration can exist because the breadth, character, and aim of interdisciplinary and transdisciplinary projects vary too widely. As a consequence, as a university teacher you need to reconsider what ingredients with regard to integration are relevant for the course, project, or question at hand, formulate appropriate learning outcomes, and think of ways to assess these learning outcomes. In other words, integration is key to interdisciplinarity and transdisciplinarity and can take on different forms while being applied to different phases or elements of a project or course.

For example, when different disciplines with their associated concepts and theories are involved in a project, these may need some level of integration to ensure that a coherent research problem is determined since the same concept may be defined very differently by different disciplines (Keestra, forthcoming). In this case, you may want to assess – among other things – the ability of students to use selected disciplinary insights in an appropriate way, to define a more comprehensive concept, or to reformulate some definitions such that they at least do not contradict each other.

If looking for ways to assess integration in the research work of students, the book *Methods for transdisciplinary research* by Bergmann et al. (2012) can be useful. This book shows a variety of methods, ingredients, and instruments for integration in different stages of the research process, including integration through conceptual clarification and theoretical framing, integration through the joint formulation of relevant research questions, and hypothesis or integration through the use and development of integrative methods. These examples show that developing a product, intervention, or prototype is a much-used method to assess integration. But as already stated before, because of the variety of manifestations and contexts of integration, a generally applicable assessment method cannot be found.

From the examples in this handbook, we distilled some learning outcomes regarding integration.

Examples of learning outcomes regarding integration
The student is able to:
- discuss the links between different sustainability solutions (example 1)
- develop an interdisciplinary research question and answer that question while bearing responsibility for the knowledge gained in one's own discipline (example 6)
- combine insights from different disciplines to understand and analyze migration-related social phenomena (example 12)

Many different strategies, methods, and tools exist to determine the extent to which students are able to integrate concepts and perspectives. In this handbook, we present six examples of integration, including a simulation game that helps students to integrate the viewpoint of different nations (example 1), a portfolio assessment developed for the purpose of assessment *for* learning (example 5), and a rubric for the assessment of integration in capstone projects (example 6).

Assessing critical thinking

In order to integrate theories, insights, and tools, students should be able to think critically within, outside, and across the various disciplines that are relevant for their course or project. Critical thinking can be described as the process of actively and analytically gathering information, content, facts, and theories, after which the student puts all the information effectively and reflectively into practice (Facione, 2011; Paul & Elder, 2007). In this book, we use the definition given by Facione (2011) in which critical thinking is divided into different subskills: ordering and structuring, reasoning, analyzing, evaluating, and sound decision-making.

Ordering and structuring information is the ability to appropriately discern main points and side issues and to reproduce and represent information in a logical and clear way. When working in an interdisciplinary team, students may have to rely on the expertise of others because they are entering relatively unknown areas. As such, it is important that students have the skills to systematically order and structure this new information. Reasoning refers to underpinning a statement with arguments or – by using assumptions – drawing inferences, referring to evidence, and using these with clarity and precision. In order for students to develop the skill of reasoning with the aim of analyzing truth claims across disciplines, they need to draw conclusions on the basis of arguments and give due consideration to all relevant factors (Ivanitskaya, Clark, Montgomery & Primeau, 2002; Nosich, 2012). Analyzing is a skill that students need in order to conceptualize an interdisciplinary problem and capture its essence in a short and concise way. It not only involves recognizing assumptions and examining the argument's logic to determine its validity but also entails the systematic breakdown of the problem into meaningful smaller components while being continuously aware of the intricate relationships between the components. Evaluation is the ability to weigh the benefits of one disciplinary perspective against those of another and against the overall purpose of the problem or question at hand (Boix Mansilla & Dawes Duraisingh, 2007). Students must be able to weigh emerging insights against one another and against prior knowledge and competing understandings (Boix Mansilla, 2010). Evaluation further entails weighing evidence: determining the validity of data-based generalizations or conclusions (Ivanitskaya et al., 2002; Terenzini & Pascarella, 1991). Sound decision-making is a skill that entails gathering and integrating information, using sound judgment, and identifying alternatives with the aim of selecting the best solution (Cannon-Bowers & Salas, 1997). Sound decision-making is the skilful, responsible thinking that is conducive to good judgment because it is sensitive to context (Nosich, 2012) and enables students to apply the integrated results to a particular context.

From the examples in this handbook, we distilled some learning outcomes regarding critical thinking.

Examples of learning outcomes regarding critical thinking
The student is able to:
- take a well-reasoned position on a sustainability issue, with ethical, economic, social, and physical aspects taken into account (example 1)
- take an informed position from the perspective of a specific stakeholder (example 4)
- analyze differences in disciplines and define common ground between potentially conflicting insights by selecting appropriate integrative techniques (example 6)

Later on in this handbook, we present six examples of critical thinking, for instance an example where students are assessed on their ability to come up with substantive ideas in class and combine insights from different disciplines to understand and analyze migration-related social phenomena.

Assessing collaboration
Collaborative work is important in the study of complex phenomena that are often key in interdisciplinary education, where students often work together in groups. The literature gives us some directions for the operationalization of interdisciplinarity group work into learning outcomes.

To achieve collective goals, members of a team must communicate effectively to construct a set of concepts and terms that bridge the team members' respective backgrounds. Developing a common language has been identified as one of the challenges of interdisciplinarity teamwork (Benda et al., 2002; Glantz & Orlovsky, 1986). Given that different disciplines frequently take conflicting views of the same situation, another challenge students face is that, in order to come to an agreement, they have to make an effort to understand each other's points of view. By doing so, they discover what models and appreciations lead each of them to focus preferentially on one set of facts or criteria and find out how one can understand the other's framing of the situation (Schön, 1987). For example, when studying attention deficit hyperactivity disorder (ADHD), insights that emerge from psychology, sociology, and biology can be integrated to come to a more comprehensive understanding of the condition. Psychologists, sociologists, and biologists have to overcome several of these challenges at the start of the integration process. The different disciplinary definitions of 'normal', 'deviant', and 'childhood' need adjustment before they can come to an integrated view on the disorder (Menken & Keestra, 2016).

Effective interdisciplinary and transdisciplinary teams comprise individuals with the knowledge needed to understand relevant specialized components and the breadth required to communicate and integrate effectively across disciplinary boundaries (O'Rourke, 2014; Morse, Nielsen-Pincus, Force & Wulfhorst, 2007; Cooke & Hilton, 2015). For students, this means that they need to reflect on theories, concepts, and methodologies that are key to their own discipline, which in turn gives rise to two questions. How have specific results in the disciplines been achieved? How have underlying assumptions, motives, and frameworks consciously or subconsciously led to these results?

In addition, collaborating students run the risk of misunderstanding each other when it comes to fundamental questions underlying the collaboration. Before a team can engage in collaborative problem-solving, it must thoroughly analyze and question definitions and terminology related to the problem. What is valid data? What kind of results or products should emerge from the project (a publication, an intervention, or perhaps a software design)? Furthermore, students – working together collectively as a team – need to develop a mental representation of the team project and its relevant components in which their individual perspectives are modified after weighing them against and integrating them with the other perspectives.

Shared values are a foundational part that drives collaborative efforts. Interdisciplinary collaboration is facilitated by the combined metacognition of team members about tasks, processes, goals, and representations they developed together and metacognition of the team itself (Keestra, 2017b).

It is important to realize that some elements of team collaboration cannot be captured in intended learning outcomes because we cannot force certain situations to actually occur. For example, a student can only show how he deals with conflicts when a conflict actually arises. Samples of learning outcomes related to collaboration are summed up below.

Examples of learning outcomes regarding collaboration
The student is able to:
- work as part of a multidisciplinary and multicultural team and value the contribution of different perspectives in designing solutions to complex (environmental) problems (example 3)
- manage a project in a professional way while making use of the team resources and diversity and cooperating with the client in a professional way (example 8)
- evaluate and critically reflect on their own contribution to the team, based on their disciplinary knowledge and academic skills (example 9)

Students do not spontaneously develop their collaboration skills without practice. Ideally, developing and assessing collaboration would occur in an authentic context, with a group of students with various cultural and academic backgrounds working together towards a shared goal, using combinations of direct observations, working notes, blogs, final outcomes, peer assessments, and/or reflective statements to document the collaborative process. In this handbook, we present three examples of assessment regarding collaboration.

Assessing reflection

Reflection is an important skill that plays a major role in any learning process and thus in interdisciplinary education. The ability to reflect is sometimes referred to as reflective functioning (Fonagy, Gergely & Jurist, 2004). Reflective functioning can be defined as the response to another person's behavior but also understanding and acting upon the perceived underlying mental states of that behavior such as beliefs, feelings, attitudes, desires, intentions, plans, and knowledge (Allen, Fonagy & Bateman, 2008; Fonagy et al., 2004).

Reflection is closely related to self-regulation and metacognition, which is the 'active, goal-directed self-control of behaviour, motivation and cognition for academic tasks' (Pintrich, 1995). Metacognitive practices increase students' abilities to transfer or adapt their learning to new contexts and tasks (Bransford, Brown & Cocking, 2000). They demonstrate this capacity by conveying a level of awareness about the subject matter. Students reflect on the tasks and contexts of different learning situations. With metacognition skills, students gain an understanding of the situations, processes, and methods that work best for them and become more independent, autonomous learners.

Assessment of reflection and metacognition can work in a wide variety of forms: talking, blogging/vlogging, journals, diaries, portfolios, letters, or formal essays. It could be said that assessment of learning can be at odds with honest and open reflection, as students may be inclined to articulate reflections that simply present 'what the teacher wants'. Assessment *for* and *as* learning fit better than assessment *of* learning in this case. In the case of assessment *of* learning, a pass/fail system can be used as an alternative to giving a grade.

From the examples in this handbook, we distilled some learning outcomes regarding reflection.

Examples of learning outcomes regarding reflection
The student is able to:
- reflect on their own functioning and contribution to the execution of a project in terms of disciplinary knowledge, academic skills, group dynamics, and intercultural setting (example 3)
- demonstrate sensitivity to moral issues followed by a moral judgment (example 5)
- guide their learning process towards their own learning goals (example 15)
- critically reflect on their own educational trajectory and assess their contributions to the co-created learning space in this course (example 16)

In this handbook, we present six examples of assessment that focus on reflection, including giving students ownership of their learning process (example 15) and a portfolio assessment focusing on interdisciplinary competences (example 20).

Case study: Learning outcomes from the course Dealing with Complex Problems: The Food Issue, BSc in Future Planet Studies, University of Amsterdam

The following example of interdisciplinary learning outcomes comes from a course called *Dealing with Complex Problems: The Food Issue*. This is a second-year bachelor's course that is part of the BSc in Future Planet Studies at the University of Amsterdam. The overall aim of this course is to help students develop a nuanced view of what science, the acquisition of knowledge, and the development of vision entail and how they can contribute to finding solutions to pressing complex issues such as the world food issue. More specifically, the student is able to:

Integration
- use a range of conceptual tools, provided by philosophy of science, to make critical analyses and evaluations in the context of an interdisciplinary and transdisciplinary study of complex issues.

Critical thinking
- recognize various models, perspectives, and paradigms and integrate them into a more comprehensive approach to complex problems, in particular the world food problem.
- apply critical thinking skills and argumentative reasoning in a debate and dialogue as well as in writing

Disciplinary grounding
- explain the role of soil quality (nutrients), substrates, and water for the production of food.
- explain the relations between fertilizers and essential mineral nutrients in relation to crop productivity.
- explain what biological processes are involved in plant diseases and traditional and modern plant breeding, including genetically modified organisms (GMOs), and acquire competencies with regard to the plant breeder's molecular toolbox in manipulating DNA.

Other skills
- apply various forms of futures thinking and vision development with regard to finding solutions to complex issues such as the food issue.

Part 2
The examples

In this part of the handbook, we describe 20 examples of good practices of interdisciplinary skills assessment that are already used in higher education, both within and outside of the Netherlands. These examples can serve as a guide for designing and implementing assessment methods in your own courses. You can adjust them to fit your own situation. Before we describe these examples, some pointers are given to help you navigate this chapter.

How to navigate the examples

The 20 examples in this chapter are presented in the same format. First, we give a short overview to help you quickly scan the most important features of the assessment. This is followed by a description of the course and the specific intended learning outcomes addressed by the assessment. We then describe the method of assessment itself and provide you with the accompanying materials such as rubrics, criteria, and relevant questions. We finish every example with an interview with a lecturer who has developed and used the format in their teaching practice.

In the short overview, you will find the most important skills, characteristics, roles, and the main purpose of the assessment that are relevant for you when choosing the most appropriate assessment method for your course.

Interdisciplinary skills: integration
collaboration
critical thinking
reflection

Characteristics: authentic assessment
the assessment is based on a real-world situation or on an actual client outside academia.

portfolio assessment
students collect their assignments, artefacts, and reflections as proof of a specific competence.

assessment with rubrics
students' performances are evaluated with a matrix that indicates the criteria used to measure whether the intended learning outcomes were reached and describes levels of quality.

assessment of group work
assessment of the outcome of the group work (product) or the process of the group working together or both.

self-regulated learning
students are metacognitively, motivationally, and behaviorally active contributors in their own learning process.

Roles: **self-assessment**
assessment in which students make judgments, reflect on, or grade their own learning process or work.

peer assessment
assessment in which students give feedback or grade their peers.

teacher-led assessment
assessment activity that is carried out by a teacher.

Purpose: **for learning**
of learning
as learning

1 Assessing perspective-taking skills with a simulation game

Interdisciplinary skills:	integration collaboration critical thinking
Characteristics:	authentic assessment assessment with rubrics assessment of group work
Roles:	peer assessment teacher-led assessment
Purpose:	of learning for learning
Course:	Global Challenges
Program:	minor in Future Planet Innovation
Institute:	University of Groningen (NL)
Study load:	280 hours
Group size:	25 students
Year:	third-year bachelor's students
Lecturer:	Jorien Zevenbergen

Sustainability issues are characterized by complexity and uncertainty. These issues call for a global and interconnected perspective. It requires students to formulate their perspective and then reflect on it in terms of their own cultural assumptions and biases. In this example, students learn to take the perspective of a certain nation on a sustainability issue, substantiate their position with arguments, integrate them, and come up with globally coordinated and integrated policy plans. The assessment is designed in the form of a simulation game to encourage students to integrate perspectives, become aware of interdependence, and be individually accountable for team success.

About the course and assessment

Brief description of the course

In the course *Global Challenges*, students play a simulation game named *i*Risk, which stands for 'inverse RISK'. The main idea of this game is not to conquer the world but to save the world by tackling global challenges together. It is a real-life game where the students imitate negotiations between the United Nations and the different continents. The course is part of the minor in Future Planet Innovations and open to all bachelor's students of the university, no matter what their major is. Student teams represent the different continents and learn how to design feasible sustainability solutions for specific regions. The course has two segments:

1. lectures in which actual topics are discussed and background information is provided from the natural sciences, social sciences, and arts as well as seminars where students play iRisk, and
2. a final day on which the student 'UN representatives' select the plans that have the highest potential to improve the world.

In the first part of the game, students are divided into groups of five that represent eight different continents (Asia is split into Central Asia, Southeast Asia, China/Korea/Japan, and the Middle East). One group of students plays the role of the United Nations. Over a period of five weeks, student teams present their plans for a better world, focusing every week on a specific topic discussed during the lectures of that week.

The student teams each have one president and four ministers (one minister for every week). The president is responsible for planning the group meetings, setting out a sustainability plan for the continent, and keeping the general overview. The ministers are all specialized in the themes of the different weeks mentioned above and have to present a sustainability plan for the topic of that specific week. The presentations are pitches that should last no more than five minutes. At the end of every session, the team that represents the United Nations gives an overview of what was presented by the different continents and presents their vision on how different plans together can contribute to a better world.

The second part of the game consists of one final meeting where the students have to negotiate with each other and where they pitch their final plans. This final meeting is called the 'congress'. During the congress, the UN team has the special role of making a selection of all the plans that were presented in the preceding weeks. It is on the day of the congress that the real political game is played. The day starts with a poster market where the continents show a poster for every plan they presented in the weeks before. There are four areas, one for each week/theme. The UN gives four pitches, one for each theme, in which they will construct a framework of their vision on which plans combined can save the world.

The intended learning outcomes of this course that are addressed in this example

The student is able to:
- explain the background of sustainability issues in context
- discuss the links between different sustainability solutions
- show the subjectivity of sustainability issues
- take a well-reasoned position on a sustainability issue with ethical, economic, social, and physical aspects taken into account

Description of the assessment

The simulation game is played in two parts: the weekly seminars and the final congress. The assessment is structured accordingly.

Receiving feedback during the weekly seminars

Every week, the student teams receive feedback on the pitch via a rubric. The staff as well as the student teams themselves fill in a feedback form using this rubric. This rubric is the same that is used at the final meeting – the congress – to grade the final presentations. In this way, the students are able to get used to the assessment criteria and understand which steps they must take to improve their work. The assembly ends with a student election of the best contribution. The winning continent gets a 'wild card' to the final round of the congress.

Final grade at the congress

The framework that the UN team presents can only include four out of the eight plans, and the winning plan from each week must be incorporated. To achieve this, students in the UN team need to use perspective-taking skills to integrate the plans into a consistent vision. The continent teams that have not been placed within the initial UN framework will need to lobby to convince the UN to change its decision. This is a very dynamic part of the day. Everyone is walking around the different posters and talking to different people to try to get their poster in the UN framework. For this activity, the continent teams also need to use perspective-taking skills. Both the framework and the plans may be adapted. After the lobbying is done, the UN gives four pitches on its final choice, one pitch for every theme it picked. The choice should be well-considered and based on the theoretical background of the plans. In total, the UN selects 16 plans, four for every theme. In order to be successful, the UN team must understand that it should involve the whole world in their selection, which in essence means picking at least one plan from each continent. The selected plans are then pitched by the continents. In the end, four winners – one for every theme – are elected by the UN.

The UN team is graded for the pitches on its final decision of the selected plans. Here the students can show they understand the implications of the different plans and how those plans combined can contribute to a more sustainable world. The continent teams are graded for the pitches they give on their selected plan (or plans). This may be one pitch or more; if the plans are better and/or they did a better job in lobbying, they will give more pitches. In the end, the plan is graded by the staff. However, in order to present the best plan, the students have to prove they can lobby and convince others. The lecturers use the same rubric as they used for the pitches in the weekly seminars.

The final mark for the whole course consists of a grade for the game (group mark, 20%) and a grade for an individual exam (80%).

Assessment materials

The grading rubric below is used both by students giving feedback on the pitches given by their fellow students in the weekly seminars (peer assessment) and by staff grading the final pitches during the congress.

Criterion	Un-satisfactory	Satisfactory	Amply sufficient	Good	Very good	Excellent
Planet / Physical system	Aspect is completely missing.	Several relevant aspects are mentioned, but they are not placed in context properly.	Mentioned arguments are relevant in the context.	Important arguments are presented in an adequate way.	All arguments are present, and they are interpreted persuasively.	Plan shows synergy.
People / Social system						
Profit / Economic system						
Ethics / Values system						
Transition / System change		Transition element is mentioned.	System change is compatible with the initial situation.	System change is compatible with the initial situation and the pros and cons are compared.	The pros and cons of system change are interpreted persuasively.	
Under-standing	Shouts instead of facts and reasoning.	Build an opinion upon facts.	Compare opinions and facts.	Take a well-balanced point of view.	Adjust point of view based on new insights.	Thourough under-standing of the system
Consistency	No attention to con-sequences.	Recognize causality.	Face the consequen-ces of own plan.	Face the consequen-ces of own plan and deal with it.	Critical reflection on plan.	After critical self-reflection still being able to sell own plan.

Experiences and insights of the lecturer
Jorien Zevenberg

The reason for using the assessment method

The interactive form of learning helps the students to integrate the many perspectives of sustainability and apply these to real-life, actual problems. By embedding the subject matter in the context of real-world challenges, student learning is transferred from the classroom to the realm of practice. Since the plans of the continents need to fit into the integrated framework of the UN, and because the UN prefers plans that help to tackle the global challenges, students learn to integrate other perspectives into their plans.

Reflections on the assessment method

We have been working with this simulation game in this course for a while now and have changed the design of the course and the rubric each year. What worked very well for our team is using a rubric for feedback during the seminars and using the same one for grading at the end of the course. This makes the assessment an ongoing effort to help students learn. First, students receive feedback from peers and staff, and then they have a second chance to demonstrate their new level of competence and understanding. Enrolling more students in the course would be a challenge because giving feedback takes time. The described course is part of a minor. The simulation is very different from the other assessment methods used in the minor. Incorporating different types of assessment strategies into the minor accommodates the various students' interests and preferences.

Advantages and disadvantages

Students find the simulation game inspiring, and the game makes authentic learning possible. Scaling up is a challenge.

Key advice
- Use the same rubric in both the feedback on the weekly pitches and the final summative assessment. This makes the students aware of the criteria, helps them to understand the criteria, and makes it possible for them to improve the content of their pitches.
- If you want to start with a simulation, our advice would be to only allocate 10% of the grade to the simulation in the pilot version of a new course. This will give you more freedom to experiment and to see how you can improve the design the next time.
- Although we have developed a rubric, it still is a good idea to discuss this with the lecturers who will grade the students, in other words, to calibrate the use of the rubric. If possible, involve the lecturers in developing the rubric.

2 Making 'big ideas' tangible with an installation

Interdisciplinary skills:	integration reflection
Characteristics:	assessment with rubrics assessment of group work
Role:	teacher-led assessment
Purpose:	of learning
Course:	Big Questions in Time
Program:	BSc in Liberal Arts and Sciences
Institute:	University of Amsterdam & VU Amsterdam (NL)
Study load:	168 hours
Group size:	25 students
Year:	second-year and third-year bachelor's students
Lecturer:	Anco Lankreijer, Joost Krijnen, and Dora Achourioti

A university teacher team at Amsterdam University College developed a course called Big Questions in Time, with the main aim of making the interdisciplinary aspect of this topic concrete and tangible for their students. The teachers opted for assignments and assessment formats that go beyond the traditional research paper, the most important of which is the construction of an installation that represents the concept of 'time' and an accompanying substantiation and motivation. As a team, the teachers developed a rubric with assessment criteria in line with the learning outcomes of the course.

About the course and assessment

Brief description of the course

Time is a central concept in our thinking but has profoundly different meanings in different disciplines. In this elective course for second-year students of the Liberal Arts and Sciences program at Amsterdam University College, students start by exploring the role of time in a number of disciplines and then comparing and contrasting these concepts to those of other disciplines. Topics include measuring time, the historical development of the concept of time, deep time, space time, time and age, time as cultural concept, and time as a social construct. Many of the problems that society faces are in some way related to time. Sustainability, for example, is closely intertwined with different perspectives on time and yields different solutions depending on the timescale used. Population increases or the depletion of resources can be viewed on a human timescale, which already has a different reality for students than it does for university teachers.

In the second part of the course, students work in interdisciplinary groups on practical projects. Students can define their own projects, provided they are of an interdisciplinary nature and will entail a practical application of their knowledge. The final products include an installation contrasting different perspectives of time that will be exhibited in a 'Big Time museum'. In an online version of the museum guests could view the students' work in a virtual tour. Creativity is a vital ingredient in the project, as students in interdisciplinary teams will build a tangible installation representing time. The project requires cooperation skills, interdisciplinary skills, and maker skills in combination with artistic skills.

The intended learning outcomes of this course that are addressed in this example
The student is able to:
- define and critically discuss time in their own disciplinary context
- critically reflect on interdisciplinarity

Description of the assessment
In this course, the exhibition group project is the central assignment. For this assignment, students will be assigned to an interdisciplinary group of four students. Together, they build an installation that presents, materializes, or concretizes an interdisciplinary perspective on time. Students can come up with an artwork, a multimedia installation, a film, or some kind of time-keeping appliance. It will be assessed using the following grading criteria: interdisciplinarity, level, alignment, clear message, creativity, and craftsmanship.

To accompany the installation, the students will write an essay (or 'catalog text') that explains the theoretical and interdisciplinary rationale informing their installation. The essay must deepen the audience's understanding of the perspective on time that the installation presents. The installation and essay should mutually reinforce each other: by viewing the installation and reading the essay in tandem, the audience should get a better understanding of both.

Assessment materials
The following rubric is developed to grade the installations.

Criterion	Insufficient	Sufficient	Good	Very good
1 Interdisciplinarity: Does the installation integrate or contrast interdisciplinary concepts about time?	The installation displays one aspect of time; other disciplinary perspectives are not present; integration of contrasting disciplines is not present.	The installation integrates or contrasts different perspectives on time. One perspective dominates; others are marginally involved.	The installation integrates or contrasts different perspectives on time. Multiple perspectives are significantly integrated or contrasted.	The installation provokes discussion of interdisciplinary aspects of time and engages deeply in either contrasting or integrating multiple different disciplinary perspectives on time.
2 Level: Does the installation display a deep understanding of concepts related to time?	The installation uses basic, pre-course notions of time.	The installation shows a basic understanding of the different disciplinary concepts of time.	The installation addresses concepts related to time in moderately advanced ways; at least one concept is used at an advanced level.	The installation shows an advanced use of concepts related to time. All involved concepts are engaged with at an advanced level.
3 Alignment: Do the installation and essay reinforce each other?	No major concepts from the essay can be recognized in the installation.	Some concepts from the essay can be recognized in the installation.	All concepts from the essay can be recognized in the installation.	All the major concepts from the essay can be recognized in the installation, and the installation materializes the concepts in the essay.

4 **Clear message:** Does the installation present a clear message, and does it engage the audience?	The intention, or message, is not clear for the audience and is open to interpretation. Concepts are hard to recognize. The installation does not trigger a reaction from the audience.	The main intention can be recognized by the audience.	The intention of the installation can be recognized by the audience. The installation provokes a reaction from the audience.	The installation has a clear message and guides the audience to understand the meaning of the installation without requiring explanation. The installation engages with the audience, elicits wonder, and makes them think in the direction intended.
5 **Creativity:** Does the installation engage with time in original and/or innovative ways?	The installation reuses existing concepts in a traditional way.	The installation shows some original ideas.	The installation shows a number of original and innovative ideas about time and goes beyond combining traditional ideas.	The installation engages with time in a very creative and innovative way, inviting the audience to think about time in unexpected ways.
6 **Craftsmanship:** Does the installation portray craftsmanship, artistry, and group collaboration?	The installation is technically and or artistically flawed. It is not the product of a collaboration involving the whole group.	The installation is technically and artistically mostly sound. The input of the group is somewhat unbalanced.	The installation is technically and artistically sound. The input of the group is balanced.	The installation is technically and artistically sophisticated. It is the product of integrative and cross-fertilizing collaboration.
7 **Open student criterion**				

Experiences and insights of the lecturer
Anco Lankreijer

The reason for using the assessment method
We were looking for a way to let students really experience the concept of time in order to understand it more deeply. Going beyond just remembering facts, we want students to undergo hands-on interdisciplinary collaboration and to learn from a transformational educational experience. We felt that constructing an installation as a group and reflecting on it together would be an accurate reflection of the kind of thinking and problem-solving we wanted our students to engage in.

Reflections on the assessment method
As a team of lecturers, we are very enthusiastic about this assignment because it has resulted in very committed students and has boosted students' motivation. The museum tour was a festive finale of the course in which we could also involve other lecturers, students, family, and friends.

Advantages and disadvantages
A major plus of this assignment was the students' engagement and enthusiasm. It worked out well for both the lecturer and the students to step out of our comfort zone. I would also consider the hands-on experience of working in an interdisciplinary group as an advantage. The only disadvantage I would mention is the significant influence that the group dynamics – i.e. whether the collaboration goes well or not – has on the end result and the grade.

> **Key advice**
> Think about exactly what it is you want to assess. Take the time to develop the assessment and rubric with the entire teaching team and discuss exactly what skills and knowledge your assessment should include. By thinking through the rubric carefully, the assignment becomes much clearer and more specific.

3 Self-assessment of boundary-crossing competences

Interdisciplinary skills:	integration collaboration reflection
Characteristics:	authentic assessment self-regulated learning
Roles:	self-assessment peer assessment teacher-led assessment
Purpose:	for learning as learning
Course:	European Workshop Environmental Sciences and Management
Program:	elective for MSc Environmental Sciences, MSc Urban Environmental Management, MSc Tourism, MSc Society and Environment, MSc Aquaculture and Marine Resource Management
Institute:	Wageningen University (NL)
Study load:	336 hours
Group size:	30 students
Year:	first-year master's students
Lecturer:	Karen Fortuin, Judith Gulikers, and Carla Oonk

Wageningen University trains students to be future experts by tackling present-day complex problems. Dealing with these kinds of issues requires crossing boundaries between people coming from different practices, disciplines, and cultures. The concept of 'boundary crossing' is used to develop students' competence to co-create new knowledge and work towards innovation or transformation for sustainable practice. Building on the boundary-crossing theory, the lecturers developed a rubric to allow students to describe their learning goals and reflect on their boundary-crossing competence development. The criteria presented in this example can be applied to all kinds of transdisciplinary student work, independent of the specific content, and as such is generically applicable to transdisciplinary projects.

About the course and assessment

Brief description of the course

The *European Workshop Environmental Sciences and Management* is an eight-week, full-time course offering students the opportunity to work on an authentic consultancy project through a collaborative interdisciplinary and/or transdisciplinary research project in an intercultural setting. A group of about 30 students of different nationalities and disciplinary backgrounds work together on an assignment commissioned by an external partner. By working on this assignment, students have to make links between various disciplines, cultures, and academic and non-academic societal partners as well as between theory and practice.

The course consists of three phases. In the preparation phase, students make a project plan based on the problem statement and question proposed by the external partner. In this period, students are offered applied training in project management, data collection, interview techniques, and teamwork. A few tailor-made lectures provide students with additional background information to tackle the issue. Furthermore, students do a self-assessment of the skills necessary to successfully conduct an interdisciplinary and intercultural project. They reflect on the skills they already possess and define their own learning goals for the course based on their previous experiences and their experience during the first three weeks of the course. The second phase consists of field work mainly dedicated to data collection. To cover the broad spectrum of the problems, the core group of 30 students is divided into subgroups. Each student participates in a variety of subgroups, such as data collection groups and expert groups, which investigate a particular aspect of the problem (technological, political, or economic). By collaborating in a variety of subgroups, students must cross boundaries in a variety of settings. A management team composed of student members coordinates the work of the overarching core group.
In the final phase, students are expected to analyze the data, incorporate the feedback from the external partner, and write a report in which the input from all the subgroups is synthesized. The lecturer's main task is to facilitate the process of the group work during the various stages of the consultancy research project.
The final mark for this course is based on a combination of students' individual performance (participation and final reflection report) and the products created by the group (subgroup reports and synthesis report). The final reflection report counts for 25% of the final mark for the course. One assessment criterion for this final reflection report is boundary crossing. In this example, we focus on this aspect. The boundary-crossing rubric is primarily intended as a tool to facilitate learning across borders and is particularly suitable for use in formative testing.

The intended learning outcomes of this course that are addressed in this example

The student is able to:
- integrate their academic knowledge and general academic skills and attitude to a project dealing with a complex problem commissioned by a partner outside the university
- work as part of a multidisciplinary and multicultural team and value the contribution of different perspectives in designing solutions to complex (environmental) problems
- reflect on their own functioning and contribution to the execution of a project in terms of disciplinary knowledge, academic skills, group dynamics, and intercultural setting

Description of the assessment

In the final reflection report (1000-2000 words), the student includes a self-assessment of their boundary-crossing competencies. At the start of the course, students fill in a self-assessment form in which they indicate at what level they think they currently operate for each performance indicator of the boundary-crossing rubric and what level they aim to reach during the course. This expectation paper is discussed with the student individually during a half-hour coaching session. At the end of the course, students assess themselves again. They have to spend a section of their reflection report on the scores that stand out the most: Did they achieve the level they aimed for or not? Why? Furthermore, they are expected to include examples of boundary-crossing learning experiences as arguments for their assessed performance levels. The finalized self-assessment form is added to their final reflection report. Students are advised to keep track of their experiences by making daily or weekly notes in a logbook. The rubric is used by the lecturers to inform students about their progress and to aid them in their development.

Assessment materials

The rubric was developed based on the theoretical framework of boundary crossing, in which boundaries between practices (different disciplines, perspectives, cultures, or societal groups) are viewed as powerful places for learning, knowledge co-creation, and innovation. Boundary-crossing theory identifies four learning mechanisms that facilitate this type of learning and innovation: (1) identification, (2) coordination, (3) perspective making and learning, and (4) transformation.

Learning catalyst 1: identification

Identification refers to identifying what expertise is needed to execute the project successfully and the limitations and contributions of the students' own expertise. The student relates his/her own expertise to that of the other members of the project team and maps out the kind of expertise that is missing (Identification 1). The student will then specify which aspects of the project he/she needs other people for and will plan actions to contact these other people (Identification 2).

Learning catalyst 2: coordination

The student knows how to contact and collaborate with other relevant people to execute the project successfully (Coordination 1). The student will then initiate and organize collaborative meetings with these people for the purpose of collaboratively sharing ideas, developing new ideas, and fine-tuning his/her own ideas (Coordination 2).

Learning catalyst 3: perspective making and learning

The student wants to learn from and with others. He/she is willing to empathize with others and to reflect on and reconsider one's own perspective and expertise. In addition, he/she stimulates others to reflect on and reconsider their expertise and practices. The student actively discusses various perspectives that are relevant for the project and searches for ways to combine perspectives (Perspective making and learning 1). The student actively searches for ways to learn from others and to develop him/herself (Perspective making and learning 2) and actively encourages other people to learn from the project (Perspective making and learning 3).

Learning catalyst 4: transformation

The student adopts an attitude of wanting to deliver a project result that is inspiring or innovative (Transformation 1). The student can convey his/her vision for the new practice, i.e. he/she can explain what the new practice would look like, how it would function, and what needs to be done to realize this new practice (Transformation 2). The student clearly explicates how to effectively inform other external people involved about the outcome of the final product (Transformation 3), and he/she shows enthusiasm and effort in being actively involved in follow-up activities (Transformation 4).

Below is the self-assessment form for boundary-crossing skills.

Performance indicator	Personal assessment
Identification 1: Identify one's own expertise and one's own limitations	start D C B A aim D C B A end D C B A
Identification 2: Identify other perspectives relevant for the project and the problem at hand	start D C B A aim D C B A end D C B A
Coordination 1: Contact other people	start D C B A aim D C B A end D C B A

Example 3 **Self-assessment of boundary-crossing competences**

Coordination 2:
Collaborate purposefully
with other people

start	D	C	B	A
aim	D	C	B	A
end	D	C	B	A

Perspective making and learning 1:
(Re)consider perspectives

start	D	C	B	A
aim	D	C	B	A
end	D	C	B	A

Perspective making and learning 2:
Learn from other people

start	D	C	B	A
aim	D	C	B	A
end	D	C	B	A

Perspective making and learning 3:
Stimulate others to learn

start	D	C	B	A
aim	D	C	B	A
end	D	C	B	A

Transformation 1 (start):
Intend to develop a new,
sustainable practice

start	D	C	B	A
aim	D	C	B	A
end	D	C	B	A

Transformation 2 (process):
Envision new practices
during the project process

start	D	C	B	A
aim	D	C	B	A
end	D	C	B	A

Transformation 3 (product):
Integrate various perspectives,
interests, or expertise into the
final product

start	D	C	B	A
aim	D	C	B	A
end	D	C	B	A

Transformation 4 (follow-up):
Stimulate a follow-up on
project results

start	D	C	B	A
aim	D	C	B	A
end	D	C	B	A

Experiences and insights of the lecturers
Karen Fortuin, Judith Gulikers, and Carla Oonk

The reason for using the assessment method

This boundary-crossing rubric was developed for three purposes: (1) to allow students to conduct an initial self-assessment on the rubric performance indicators and to set personal learning goals; (2) to coach student groups while learning and working together in their multidisciplinary and multicultural groups and with various external stakeholders; and (3) to allow students to reflect on their boundary-crossing learning after completing the project. The principle behind this rubric is that students can measure their development and get feedback from their lecturers during a coaching session rather than be judged or graded by the lecturer.

Reflections on the assessment method

In the first year that we introduced the rubric, we noticed that it was difficult for students to understand the instrument and to set specific learning goals regarding 'working with the other.' It took a few years before the rubric was properly embedded in the course. But we now see that students realize that boundaries do not hamper their learning but instead may offer powerful learning opportunities (e.g. 'I never realized that students from another discipline can view a problem so differently than I do.'). More than before, students realize that presenting their results to an external commissioner has different requirements than writing an academic report. And since boundary crossing is more explicitly addressed during the course and more often talked about during coaching, students' reflection reports on their boundary-crossing development are much richer and more specific than in previous cohorts.

Advantages and disadvantages

The rubric allows university teachers to explicitly value the boundary crossing attitude of the students. It helps the lecturers give words to their observations. Using the rubric in our teaching and coaching has been difficult, and it has been even more challenging to help new lecturers to use the boundary-crossing concepts in their teaching. University teachers are not used to looking at student attitudes and performances in this way or coaching them to learn from people and concepts beyond their boundary. That is why we are developing a university teacher course on boundary crossing so that lecturers can use it optimally in their coaching of student groups.

Key advice
Use the boundary crossing rubric as a formative tool. What is most important is that students are able to describe experiences using concrete examples, behavior, and experiences. It is important for them to grasp and monitor the development in their competence and not focus on the achieved level. Make boundary crossing explicit in the course design by introducing the theory, implementing learning activities, and referring to boundary crossing in the coaching of students.

Further readings
  Gulikers, J.T.M. and Oonk, C., (2019). Towards a Rubric for Stimulating and Evaluating Sustainable Learning. *Sustainability*, 11 (4), 969.
  Gulikers, J.T.M. and Oonk, C., (2016). Het leren waarderen van leren met partijen buiten de school. *Onderwijsinnovatie*, 17-26.
  Akkerman, S.F., & Bakker, A. (2011). Boundary Crossing and Boundary Objects. *Review of educational research*, 81(2), 132-169.

4 Peer feedback on the reflection of a stakeholder dialogue

Interdisciplinary skills:	integration reflection
Characteristics:	authentic assessment assessment of group work
Roles:	self-assessment peer assessment teacher-led assessment
Purpose:	for learning of learning
Course:	Spatial Programming & Design
Program:	BSc in Social Geography and Planning
Institute:	University of Amsterdam (NL)
Study load:	168 hours
Group size:	120 students
Year:	first-year bachelor's students
Lecturer:	Nanke Verloo

Students of interdisciplinary and transdisciplinary study programs are trained to work in a professional setting with diverse stakeholders, cultures, knowledge sources, and experiences. They must develop the ability to integrate new knowledge, cooperate within diverse groups, deal with conflicts among stakeholders, and find creative ways to communicate complex issues. In this example, students experience a stakeholder dialogue in a case with conflicting interests by taking the perspective of one of the stakeholders. Peer assessment is used to improve students' reflection on their integration and negotiation skills.

About the course and assessment

Brief description of the course

In the course *Spatial Programming & Design*, first-year bachelor's students learn how to design and restructure an area of the city or region. Municipalities act as external partners and provide a case study of an area they are planning to restructure in the near future, giving the students a specific spatial challenge to tackle. For example, in 2016, one municipality asked the students to make a spatial design that could be a solution to the high number of vacant office buildings in the area around their railway station.

At the start of the course, students are divided into groups, with each group representing a stakeholder in the urban development problem at hand. Stakeholders may include the municipality, the social housing corporation, local schools, neighborhood representatives, project developers, or local business owners, depending on the specific case study. Throughout the course, each group acts as the assigned stakeholder. Working with external partners on an actual case makes it authentic and very rewarding.

The course is divided into four weeks. In Week 1, students perform a stakeholder analysis in which they investigate who the stakeholders are and what their exact interests are. They use a so-called power-interest grid and a stakeholder outline to map out the stakeholders and their interests and strategies. They also make a stakeholder-commitment matrix to clarify the position of each party relative to the project, which makes clear what their party should negotiate for to make the project a success. How do the parties view each other and what kind of relationship do they have with each other? In Week 2, the students make their initial designs based on the interests and perspective of the stakeholder they represent. In Week 3, the students negotiate their designs and interests with the other stakeholder groups in a two-hour-long negotiation roleplay simulation. The goal of this roleplay is for the stakeholder groups to secure their particular interests with the perspectives of the other parties in mind. In the final week, students finalize and present their urban development plan to actual civil servants of the municipality and offer a feasibility assessment of their design based on the outcomes of the negotiation.

The intended learning outcomes of this course that are addressed in this example

The student is able to:
- design an urban development plan using an integral group exercise (stakeholder analysis and simulation)
- take an informed position from the perspective of a specific stakeholder, negotiate on behalf of this stakeholder, and reflect on their position in relation to the other stakeholders involved

Description of the assessment

The final assessment of the course is the group's spatial program and plan. This report includes the stakeholder analysis, the reflection assignment on the negotiation, the designs, the feasibility assessment, and the visual plans. The simulation itself is not assessed, but the reflection on the simulation is assessed based on a reflection assignment. The quality of the reflection is assessed in three steps.

Step 1: Self-reflection
The students write an individual reflection report on how the negotiation simulation played out for the stakeholder they represented.

Step 2: Peer feedback
The report is given to another student group representing a different stakeholder. The student groups peer-review each other's reports and must not only write down their feedback but also consider whether reading the reflection report of another group affects their view of their own position as a stakeholder.

Step 3 Teacher-led assessment
The lecturer of the course gives oral feedback on the peer feedback report. In commenting on the reflection and peer review, the lecturer pays attention to whether students can describe and analyze their own role in the simulation and whether they achieved a feeling for where conflicts arise with other stakeholders and showed understanding for the diversity of different perspectives. This results in a grade.

Assessment materials

The students in the different stakeholder groups are assigned to read the reflection report of other groups and give peer feedback. Below are the instructions given to the students for peer feedback.

Instructions for peer feedback	Feedback
Mention which parts of the reflection are the most informative and interesting to you and why.	
Describe which parts of the reflection surprise you and why, being specific and mentioning why this perspective is different from that of your group.	
Look for comments that mark underlying assumptions, for example, 'if there are too many renting inhabitants living in the area, the entrepreneurs will not earn enough', then explain what the underlying assumption of such sentences is and give arguments to substantiate or question the assumption.	
Ask a question that will make the group who wrote the reflection think about their perspective.	

Experiences and insights of the lecturer
Nanke Verloo

The reason for using the assessment method

The reason we incorporated a simulation into this course was to make students experience the planning process from the actual perspective of different stakeholders. By stepping into the shoes of a specific stakeholder – the municipality, a developer, a citizen, a social housing corporation – students are able to get a much more nuanced and in-depth understanding of the challenges these groups face in a planning process. Also, by experiencing a negotiation in real life, students are able to practice developing arguments and strategies to make their interests come across and convince others.

Reflections on the assessment method

Because all of this is group work, students receive one grade as a group. Generally speaking, students do not like being assessed as a group. In this course, we offer students the possibility of redistributing the given points if the group feels that some members have contributed more to the given grade than others. This can only be done in close coordination with the workgroup teacher and if all members of the team agree. In that case, the lecturer will change the grade accordingly. For example, if a group of four students receives a 7 for their final paper, that would be 28 points in total for the group (7 times 4), which can be redistributed according to the actual workload. The two who did the most work might receive an 8, in which case the two others would receive a 6 (adding up to 28 points). After agreeing, the students will email this redistribution to the lecturer, with all group members copied on the email.

Advantages and disadvantages

The three steps in the reflection assignment give students more than one opportunity to 'get it', since they have not only their own reflection but also the peer feedback as well as the lecturer's comments. The disadvantage is that designing a good simulation takes time. While the basics of a simulation can be used each year, the game must be adapted to the case study being used.

Key advice
When using simulation and reflection as an assessment activity, it is of the utmost importance to be well prepared, since the quality of the simulation determines the quality of the assessment. The best way to be prepared is to play the simulation game with the lecturers in advance. This makes it possible to find the meaningful points of negotiation and to see where conflicts could arise between the stakeholders, in particular those conflicts that are difficult to solve and force students to identify the interests behind the positions and to search for shared interests.

5 Experiencing the learning process using a portfolio

Interdisciplinary skills:	integration reflection
Characteristics:	authentic assessment portfolio assessment
Roles:	self-assessment teacher-led assessment
Purpose:	for learning as learning
Course:	Embrace Technology Entrepreneurship and Creativity
Program:	minor Embrace Technology Entrepreneurship and Creativity
Institute:	Fontys Hogeschool (NL)
Study load:	840 hours
Group size:	35 students
Year:	third-year bachelors' students
Lecturer:	Marjoleine Boersma

This example provides insight into a portfolio assessment that has been developed and used for the purpose of assessment for learning. For each learning outcome, students need to describe their learning progress in relation to the particular learning outcome. This portfolio helps students to reflect on their current situation and guide them towards where they aim to be.

About the course and assessment

Brief description of the course

The aim of this minor is for students to contribute to a better world using technology and the power of collaboration in an international team consisting of diverse disciplinary backgrounds. The student team first chooses a challenge (for example in the area of energy, environment, health, food, security, water, or sustainability). The students apply their knowledge, skills, and experience within different contexts and are guided during a design-based approach (following the model of design-based learning).

The autonomy of the students and their intrinsic motivation for the creative process are important. The students need to take ownership of the process. Step by step, they work towards a community-ready solution. During the twenty weeks of the minor, a number of ungraded feedback moments occur (based on rubrics). Information about processes and products are then uploaded to a portfolio. After eight weeks, the first formative assessment takes place based on the portfolio and the rubrics. At the end of the minor, a summative assessment takes place based on the portfolio, in combination with a performance assessment. During the second half of the minor, the students will formulate three to five personal learning goals that they really want to work on for their personal development.

One of the building blocks of the minor is a talent-based approach in which students discover their unique talent and then use it to give shape to their ultimate future solution in order to have an impact on society. To this end, over the course of 20 weeks, the students receive intensive, individual guidance by a coach.

The intended learning outcomes of this course that are addressed in this example
The student is able to:
- demonstrate their individual creative potential
- show they have an entrepreneurial attitude
- transfer a global challenge into a concrete technological application
- act as a professional partner in a multidisciplinary team
- demonstrate how their creative and innovative skills have developed
- analyze different perspectives with regard to the impact of technology on human life
- demonstrate development of ethical skills based on global citizenship
- demonstrate sensitivity to moral issues followed by a moral judgment

Description of the assessment
Students are assessed with a portfolio. They receive the following instructions to make sure their portfolio contains all the information needed to evaluate their learning process.

For each learning outcome, students need to:
1. Describe their learning progress in relation to the particular learning outcome (see table below). The guiding question is: 'What did you learn, and how?', with evidence to support their claim of progress.
2. Show that they are proficient within each indicator and refer to the supporting evidence.
3. Describe how they have applied the learning outcome in their process or product, how they plan to use it in their future professional careers, and what future goals they have related to this learning outcome.

Assessment materials

The table below shows an overview of the learning outcomes and their indicators.

Learning outcomes	Indicators
1 Identity Based on your own unique personality, you consciously and respectfully make use of the diversity and uniqueness of others while collaborating.	You can describe your talents and limitations. You can explain your personal effectiveness and your impact on other people. You can describe the situations in which your limitations arise.
2 Creativity You create and stimulate opportunities to solve complex issues using creativity. Furthermore, you understand different forms of creativity and how they lead to concrete, workable solutions.	You can apply a variety of strategies to promote the creative process of yourself and others and evaluate the effectiveness of each chosen strategy. You can express your creative process in various ways and appreciate how others express their process. You can explain your own unique creative possibilities (and limitations) and facilitate them accordingly.
3 Entrepreneurship You use your entrepreneurial attitude in formal and everyday life collaborations, characterized by a solution-oriented and action-oriented approach. You validate the impact and feasibility of your solution in the appropriate context.	You can describe the experience you gained in terms of roles and responsibilities from working together in result-oriented teams. You connect stakeholders in an active way to work together on your solution. You validate the impact of your solution in the appropriate context.
4 Technology You explore new technological applications with a design-based approach and choose the optimal role of technology in your solution by critically analyzing the options.	You develop a lasting research strategy to keep identifying new technologies. You playfully teach yourself the operation and application of technology.
5 Global citizenship You are able to communicate effectively and appropriately in intercultural situations based on your 'intercultural knowledge, skills and attitudes' (Deardorff, 2006).	You consider alternative ideas and opinions valuable and are willing to reflect on this. You develop an understanding of your frame of reference (your worldview) and are able to link this to the viewpoints of others.

The portfolio must include the following elements and cannot be graded unless all elements are present:

- **Transparency**: Students must use input and feedback from others to support their evidence. They have to know and communicate the difference between facts and opinions.
- **Evidence**: Students must provide evidence to support their claims of learning progress and refer to the appropriate pieces.
- **Completeness**: The portfolio must include all learning outcomes and all basic indicators per learning outcome.

At the end of the minor, the assessor determines whether the student's progress in learning related to the five categories of learning outcomes is insufficient (0 points), sufficient (1 point), or very good (2 points) and whether the student's proficiency related to the learning outcomes and the way in which students showed how they applied their knowledge and skills to the process and products were insufficient, sufficient, or very good.

Description	Very good 2 points	Sufficient 1 point	Insufficient 0 points
Learning Progress	The student challenged him/herself on this learning outcome, put in extra effort, and had many valuable learning experiences. And the student meets the Sufficient description. I C E T G	The student made sufficient learning progress related to the learning outcome. And the student provided sufficient evidence to support the described progress. I C E T G	The student: I did not make learning progress related to this learning outcome; or T wasn't transparent; or L did not provide enough supporting evidence. I C E T G
Basic Level	It is clear that the student has beyond-basic proficiency within one or more indicators. And the student meets the Sufficient description. I C E T G	It is clear that the student has basic proficiency within all three indicators. And the student discusses each indicator and refers to the supporting evidence. I C E T G	The student: I did not show a basic level of proficiency; or T was not transparent; or E did not provide (enough) supporting evidence; or C did not discuss all three basis indicators I C E T G
Ownership	The student explained the relevance of this learning outcome to his/her professional future and identified directions for his/her future development. And the student meets the Sufficient description. I C E T G	The student explained how the developed knowledge and skills within the learning outcome were applied to his/her process or products. I C E T G	The student did not: I explain how the developed knowledge and skills within the learning outcome were applied to his/her process or products. I C E T G
Total	I = C =	E = T =	G =
Pass	I = Pass C = Pass	E = Pass T = Pass	G = Pass
	I=Identity C=Creativity E=Entrepreneurship T=Technology G=Global Citizenship		

Experiences and insights of the lecturer
Marjoleine Boersma

The reason for using the assessment method

In this minor, it is important to give students room to develop and to experience their own way of learning because learning is not the same for everyone. This portfolio assessment provides students with the freedom they need, and it provides us – the lecturers – with much more information than a detailed snapshot of what a student knows on a particular day.

Reflections on the assessment method

We noticed that when students are more involved in designing their own learning experiences, they end up having a better grasp of the goal of the lessons and are more attached to the learning outcomes. A portfolio can contribute to this, but it is still important for this freedom to be embedded within a prescribed structure for the course.

Advantages and disadvantages

Because students can decide for themselves how to build their portfolio (e.g. with lab reports or presentations), it is more than just an administrative act for them. This form of assessment is part of their learning process. How students evaluate their portfolio assessment differs from person to person. In the *Embrace Technology Entrepreneurship and Creativity* minor, we have many students who are not used to this assessment method, and some of them prefer a fixed picture of when you are successful.

From the university teacher's perspective, it can be a joy to examine the beautiful portfolios that students hand in. It is very rewarding work to assess these. The disadvantage is that you spend a lot of time on the assessment, especially with large student numbers.

Key advice
- It is important to communicate at the beginning of the course the rules of the portfolio assessment, the success criteria, and the limits to students' freedom on this project. Students who don't understand what they are supposed to do tend to revert to a superficial approach and may end up reproducing material. If there is too much freedom and hardly no feed-up, students may think that they are doing well and can be very surprised if the lecturer is not satisfied with the end result.
- Look very carefully at what you want to achieve with the portfolio. Simply copying what you have used in other courses will not always work out well. It is important to keep developing this portfolio assessment because the students and the context of the course are constantly changing.

6   A rubric for interdisciplinary capstone projects

Interdisciplinary skills: integration   collaboration

Characteristics: assessment with rubrics   assessment of group work

Role: teacher-led assessment

Purpose: of learning

Course: Interdisciplinary Project

Program: BSc in Future Planet Studies

Institute: University of Amsterdam (NL)

Study load: 168 hours

Group size: 180 students

Year: third-year bachelor's students

Lecturer: Coyan Tromp

Rubrics are thought to be a valuable tool for monitoring students' progress and for a didactic approach in which assessment and instruction are more integrated. This example shows how a rubric is used in the setting of an interdisciplinary research project and the challenges the lecturers encountered during their teaching.

About the course and assessment

Brief description of the course

The *Interdisciplinary Project* is the final course of the bachelor's program in Future Planet Studies. After an introduction to the interdisciplinary research process that it involves, students start to work in teams on the design and execution of their interdisciplinary research project. The students must pick one of the cases that are selected by the lecturers. The cases are related to the research fields of water, food, and sustainability issues. Every case the students can choose from contains a challenge, possible solutions, and suggestions for quantitative analysis. They also contain some background literature. As a team, they develop an interdisciplinary research question. Individually, they deliver a contribution from their own discipline (the major they are following). This Individual Literature Report includes an overview of the relevant theory and literature on the chosen subject and the relevant data that are available. As a team, the students bring out a report on the research. Each team presents its research report to a broad audience during the concluding symposium. Throughout the project, the students are supervised by a university teacher with regard to the overall process and by a senior researcher who makes sure the academic quality of the project is sound.

The intended learning outcomes of this course that are addressed in this example

The student is able to:
- design and execute interdisciplinary research in an interdisciplinary team, integrating knowledge from various disciplines and producing new insights with regard to complex actual issues
- mutually develop an interdisciplinary research question and answer that question while bearing responsibility for the knowledge gained in one's own discipline
- learn how to identify the relevant (sub)disciplines and select and use disciplinary literature and knowledge (empirical data and theories) related to the research question
- augment the insights into the differences between disciplines with regard to their use of theories, concepts, models, and, to a somewhat lesser degree, their methods and techniques
- gain experience with the creation of new interdisciplinary knowledge by combining and integrating input from various disciplines
- identify differences in disciplines that can form barriers to interdisciplinary cooperation
- analyze those differences and try to define common ground between potentially conflicting insights by selecting appropriate integrative techniques
- write a report and present the research results to an academic jury

Description of the assessment

The Interdisciplinary Project consists of various assignments that are both individual and group assignments. The final mark for this course is based on students' individual reports (25%), the research proposal (group work, 10%), the final research report (group work, 55%), and the presentation (group work, 10%). In this example, we focus on the final research report. In this final product, the additional value of the interdisciplinary approach must be clearly expressed along with the social relevance of the research they have undertaken. The research proposal and the final research report are assessed using the same rubric.

Assessment materials

The following grading rubric was developed for the interdisciplinary capstone projects.

Categories	Advanced	Competent	Intermediate	Novice
Problem and topic (5%)	The topic description and relevance are clear and supported by a broad overview of relevant literature, which is critically reviewed and comprehensively argued.	The topic description and relevance are presented in a clear manner and are supported by adequate relevant literature and argumentation.	The topic description and the relevance are clear, but they are not substantiated by adequate support from relevant literature.	The topic description and the relevance are unclear and unsubstantiated and do not contain an identifiable relevance.
	The description and explanation of the complexity of the chosen wicked/interdisciplinary problem are clear and thoroughly supported by literature and by comprehensive argumentation.	The description and explanation of the complexity of the chosen wicked/interdisciplinary problem are presented in a clear manner and supported by adequate relevant literature and argumentation.	The complexity of the chosen wicked/interdisciplinary problem may be identified but is unclearly described or missing adequate argumentation.	The complexity of the chosen wicked/interdisciplinary problem remains largely implicit; the argumentation is lacking, indicating little awareness of the relevance of this complexity for the topic.
Research question and inter-disciplinarity (10%)	The research question is made perfectly clear, relevant, anchored, researchable, and precise. The research question is well-aligned with the problem description and theoretical framework.	The research question is generally clear, relevant, anchored, researchable, and precise and largely corresponds to the problem description and theoretical framework.	Either the research question is moderately clear, relevant, anchored, researchable, and precise but there is no clear connection between the problem description, the research question, and the theoretical framework, or the other way around.	The research question is not clear, relevant, anchored, researchable, and precise and/or the question is presented inconsistently. No connection is provided between the problem description and the theoretical framework.
	The purpose of the work is perfectly clear, and the relevance of the discipline(s) and the relevance of using an interdisciplinary approach are thoroughly supported by literature and comprehensive argumentation. The interdisciplinarity of the research question is very well articulated and/or expanded beyond the usual number of disciplines in an original and well-founded way.	The purpose of the work is clear, and the relevance of the discipline(s) and the relevance of using an interdisciplinary approach are supported by adequate relevant literature and argumentation.	Either the purpose of the work and the interdisciplinary character are adequately presented but the relevance of the specific disciplines is vague, or the other way around.	The interdisciplinary approach necessary for the research question is hardly developed or remains implicit. The purpose of the work is unclear, and the relevance of the disciplines and the relevance of using an interdisciplinary approach are not identified.

Example 6 **A rubric for interdisciplinary capstone projects**

Theoretical background (20%)	Selected disciplinary perspectives or insights from several disciplinary traditions are described well and systematically and clearly connected to the purpose of the work.	Selected disciplinary perspectives or insights from several disciplinary traditions are adequately described and generally balanced on substantive grounds in light of the purpose of the work.	The work shows an attempt to balance perspectives, but this is built on assumptions that are taken for granted rather than explicitly justified positions.	The work is highly biased by an imbalance in the way particular disciplinary perspectives are presented in light of the purpose of the work.	
	Grounded upon a well-developed theoretical framework; a novel, imaginative, or well-articulated integrative device (e.g. an original metaphor, a new complex causal explanation, or a newly developed theory expansion or concept extension) is used to bring disciplinary insights together in a coherent and effective way.	Loosely connected to a theoretical framework; an integrative device (e.g. a leading metaphor, a complex causal explanation, or an advanced example of theory expansion or concept extension) is used to bring disciplinary insights together in a coherent and effective way.	The topic is explored in a holistic way; however, disciplinary concepts, theories, or perspectives are placed side by side with no overall coherent integration provided, despite connections and analogies being made.	The topic is explored in a holistic way, but connections are unclear and there is no obvious effort towards integration of the various perspectives.	
Methodology (20%)	The choice for the research approach is original and is made explicit, follows logically from the theoretical framework, and is perfectly adequate to answer the research questions.	The choice for the research approach is justified and adequate in relation to the theoretical framework and sufficiently covers the research questions.	While the choice for the research approach may be justified and adequate in relation to the theoretical framework, it actually does not sufficiently cover the research questions.	The choice for the proposed research approach is unclear and is not adequate in relation to the theoretical framework and research questions.	
	The description and justification of the methods and the interdisciplinary process / technique are very clear and substantiated by comprehensive argumentation.	The description and justification of the methods and the interdisciplinary process / technique are adequate.	The description of the methods and the interdisciplinary process / technique are adequate, but the justifications and actual use are vague and incomplete, or the other way around.	A critical justification of the chosen design set-up and research methods is lacking, and the description of the methods is incomplete, resulting in vague operationalizations.	

Results and application of integrative technique (25%)	There is a rich and convincing set of data collected according to multiple and/or interdisciplinary methodologies and presented in a logical and systematic manner. The analyses are performed very well, using advanced methods. The interpretation of the results is original and well-founded and critically adds to the existing data and literature.	It is clear where the data come from and they are presented in a systematic manner. The analyses are performed adequately. The interpretation of the results is generally substantiated by relevant data and argumentation.	It is generally clear where the data come from or they are presented in a systematic manner. The analyses used are not entirely appropriate or they are incomplete. The interpretation of the results is inadequately substantiated by the provided data or is more descriptive than analytical.	Data collection is weak in that not all disciplines are equally explored for data acquisition and/or analysis and interpretation. It is unclear how the data are obtained or not enough data are presented. The data analyses are inappropriate or missing. The interpretation of the results is generally lacking or hardly substantiated.
	The results provide clear and complete answers to the research questions, as an adequate and original common ground has been identified and a fitting integrative technique has been properly applied to integrate results, leading to valuable new insights.	Through the use of an integrative technique, the results provide coherent and sufficient answers to the research questions.	Disciplinary results are put side by side; connections are made but no coherent integration is attained, resulting in incomplete answers to some or all of the research questions.	A common ground has not sufficiently been explored, nor has an integrative technique been applied to overcome differences / conflicts between perspectives, resulting in a lack of answers to some or all of the research questions.
Conclusion and critical discussion (10%)	The conclusions are systematically presented and well-founded. A proper reflection and critical assessment are provided and supported by comprehensive argumentation. In the presentation of the new-found insights, the complexity of the problem is fully taken into account, as are the merits of the interdisciplinary approach.	The conclusions are systematically presented and generally well-founded. The limitations of the project are discussed, and the results are placed in perspective using good argumentation.	The conclusions largely concur with the results but are presented in an incoherent manner. There is some critical reflection, i.e. some limitations of the project are mentioned, but they are not properly prioritized or adequately discussed.	The conclusions do not really concur with the results, and there is hardly any reflection on the limitations of the project.

	Well-substantiated, useful, and specific recommendations are provided regarding the relevant research field(s), the theoretical field(s), and/or practical applications of the obtained insights.	Adequately substantiated and specific recommendations are provided regarding the relevant research field(s), the theoretical field(s), or practical applications of the obtained insights.	Some reflection on the practical or theoretical consequences of the research and resulting recommendations are presented, but they are not supported by adequate argumentation or are not in line with the results of the research, or it is unclear to whom they are addressed.	There may be some minimal reflection on the practical or theoretical consequences of the research, but it is unclear what this is based on. Recommendations are missing or it is unclear who is to benefit from them.
Process (10%)	The contributions of all group members were well-balanced. The assignments were submitted on time and more than met all necessary requirements. The working attitude was good, and the group showed initiative and independent problem-solving skills. The guidance and feedback were optimally used, also when extra guidance was sought.	Generally, the contributions of all group members were balanced. Assignments were submitted on time and fulfilled most if not all requirements. The group asked for support in a timely manner when (extra) guidance was needed and made good use of the offered feedback.	The contributions of the group members were somewhat unbalanced. Though they generally met most of the requirements for the assignments, the submittal was sometimes too late, or there were missing parts. The group was slow in communicating when they needed (extra) support or guidance and could have made better use of the offered feedback.	The contributions of the group members were unbalanced. Generally, the submitted assignments were sloppy, handed in too late, or not handed in at all. The group failed to ask for support when (extra) guidance was needed, and no obvious use was made of the provided feedback.

Experiences and insights of the lecturer
Coyan Tromp

The reason for using the assessment method

We have developed this rubric because we thought that it could enhance the assessment process within the course. The rubric was a replacement of the more conventional method of assessment, which consisted of a list of criteria that the deliverables had to meet. We hoped that the transparency offered by the rubric would help students to take ownership of their own learning process.

Reflections on the assessment method

The introduction of the rubric has not been without objection and critique on the part of the lecturer team. Filling in the rubric felt like an enormous amount of extra work for the lecturers because the feedback they normally gave did not fit into the categories of the rubric. Part of the problem seemed to be that the rubric cannot contain many criteria that refer to topic-specific components or disciplinary knowledge (because of the interdisciplinary nature of the projects). So the lecturers felt the need to provide additional substantive feedback. For next year, we redesigned the rubric in order to ensure a fruitful use without leading to additional workload. Furthermore, we added a rough grade to each performance category and included a row under each category where university teachers can provide a more custom-made explanation of the score given for that particular task. More than last year, we need to introduce and explain how we work with the rubric – both for the junior lecturers and the expert supervisors. We also need to collect samples of student work that exemplify each performance level or at least one that is excellent and one that is clearly insufficient. I think it is worthwhile to extend our pilot and improve the use of the rubric.

Advantages and disadvantages

What I find a real threat surrounding the use of rubric is that it can easily lead to the undesired side effect of merely enhancing the extrinsically driven performance orientation that many students have. What does seem clear to me is that it may take quite comprehensive interventions in order to get the most out of the rubric.

Key advice
- Don't start using rubrics as an assessment method in the final phase of the bachelor's program but start earlier so students are familiar with the criteria and descriptors. The more they know what is expected of them, the better they are able to adjust their learning process.
- It is crucial to introduce the rubric properly to the lecturers who will be working with it and give them samples of excellent and insufficient work to help grasp what quality student work is.

7 Making failure a learning tool for collaboration skills

Interdisciplinary skills:	collaboration reflection
Characteristics:	authentic assessment assessment with rubrics self-regulated learning
Roles:	self-assessment peer assessment teacher-led assessment
Purpose:	for learning as learning
Course:	Applied Physics
Program:	BA/BSc in Engineering
Institute:	Harvard University (US)
Study load:	392 hours
Group size:	80 students
Year:	first-year bachelor's students
Lecturer:	Eric Mazur

In professional life, graduates often need to collaborate or work with others to complete tasks and projects. Having teamwork skills and experience will make it a much better experience and is a valued skill for most jobs. Therefore, this first-year course for Engineering students uses a team and project-based approach. In this approach, students can strengthen their collaborative skills, learn to give and receive peer feedback, and at the same time have the opportunity to further develop their interpersonal skills in a diverse ensemble of people. The development of collaborative skills is embedded in an assessment system and didactical approach that promote self-directed learning.

About the course and assessment

Brief description of the course

Applied Physics 50 (AP50) is a year-long course for Engineering and premedical students. It is a calculus-based introduction to physics with the aim of providing students with insight into how science applies to the real world and to teach students skills that are useful for their future career such as self-directed learning, problem-solving skills, scientific reasoning, and collaborative and communication skills. The course is designed with these goals as a central tenet and consists of three month-long projects, each culminating in a project fair at the end of the month. An example of a project is where students learn through experiments how sensors in a mobile phone can be used to record data – from tracking movements to analyzing waves. To promote self-directed learning, students are encouraged to take responsibility for their own learning process. The assignment system is flexible, and students partly determine when they do activities and when and how they are assessed. This example focuses on the assessment of contributing effectively within teams. The development of these skills is part of an assessment system where there are no final exams to grade the overall performance of students. Instead, students' work is assessed throughout the course and graded using an innovative approach called specification classification (based on Nilson & Stanny, 2014).

The intended learning outcomes of this course that are addressed in this example

The student is able to engage in productive teamwork by:
- contributing effectively in a variety of roles on diverse teams
- engage in productive teamwork by conveying information and ideas effectively using written, oral, and visual and graphical communication

Description of the assessment

This example focuses on the assessment of contributing effectively within teams. Students receive feedback on where they need to improve and can use this timely feedback to guide their learning process. To provide students with anonymized feedback on the effectiveness of their team, they receive an online assessment three times during each semester. They give feedback to all team members (including themselves) on all five criteria of the Comprehensive Assessment of Team Member Effectiveness (CATME) teamwork dimensions.

Assessment materials

Students are encouraged to use their best endeavors to accurately assess each team member's contribution to teamwork (including themselves) and to use the CATME rating scale below for this. This scale clearly and concisely describes the assessment criteria for each teamwork dimension. In the first column of the rubric, criteria or teamwork dimensions are described. The rating scale (1 = low score, 5 = high score) is given in the remaining columns. For each criterion, descriptors specify the type of behavior that matches scores 1, 3, and 5. Sores 2 and 4 are intermediate scores and are applied when students exhibit behavior that falls between descriptors 1 and 3 or between 3 and 5.

Criteria	1	2	3	4	5
Contributing to the team's work	Does not do a fair share of the team's work. Delivers sloppy or incomplete work.	*	Completes a fair share of the team's work with acceptable quality.	*	Does more or higher-quality work than expected.
			Keeps commitments and completes assignments on time.		Makes important contributions that improve the team's work.
			Helps teammates who are having difficulty when it is easy or important.		Helps teammates who are having difficulty completing their work.
Interacting with teammates	Interrupts, ignores, bosses, or makes fun of teammates.		Listens to teammates and respects their contributions.		Asks for and shows an interest in teammates' ideas and contributions.
	Takes actions that affect teammates without their input. Does not share information.		Communicates clearly. Shares information with teammates.		Makes sure teammates stay informed and understand each other.
	Complains, makes excuses, or does not interact with teammates.		Participates fully in team activities.		Provides encouragement or enthusiasm to the team.
	Is defensive. Will not accept help or advice from teammates.		Respects and responds to feedback from teammates.		Asks teammates for feedback and uses their suggestions to improve.
Keeping the team on track	Is unaware of whether the team is meeting its goals.		Notices changes that influence the team's success.		Watches conditions affecting the team and monitors the team's progress.
	Does not pay attention to teammates' progress.		Knows what everyone on the team should be doing and notices problems.		Makes sure that teammates are making appropriate progress.
	Avoids discussing team problems, even when they are obvious.		Alerts teammates or suggests solutions when the team's success is threatened.		Gives teammates specific, timely, and constructive feedback.

Expecting quality	Satisfied even if the team does not meet assigned standards.	Encourages the team to do good work that meets all requirements.	Motivates the team to do excellent work.
	Wants the team to avoid work, even if it hurts the team.	Wants the team to perform well enough to earn all available rewards.	Cares that the team does outstanding work, even if there is no additional reward.
	Doubts that the team can meet its requirements.	Believes that the team can fully meet its responsibilities.	Believes that the team can do excellent work.
Having related knowledge, skills, and abilities	Missing basic qualifications needed to be a member of the team.	Demonstrates sufficient knowledge, skills, and abilities to contribute to the team's work.	Demonstrates the knowledge, skills, and abilities to do excellent work.
	Unable or unwilling to develop knowledge or skills to contribute to the team.	Acquires knowledge or skills as needed to meet requirements.	Acquires new knowledge or skills to improve the team's performance.
	Unable to perform any of the duties of other team members.	Able to perform some of the tasks normally done by other team members.	Able to perform the role of any team member if necessary.

To meet the peer evaluation specifications (earn an M on the so-called EMRN scale), students must receive an average score of 3 or higher from their team members in each of the teamwork dimensions (details in the table below). The EMRN scale (figure 3, introduction page 17) gives students more nuanced feedback on their performance than a binary pass or fail. An E (E= exceptional) or an M (M= meets expectations) means that the work of the students meets the expectations set for that specific unit and an R (R=revision required) or an N (N=not assessable) that the work does not yet meet the specifications. At the end of the semester, the final grade can be calculated based on the number of assignments for which the students meet the specifications (D=6, C=8, B=12, and A=14).

Teamwork dimension	E	M	R	S
Contributing to the team's work	score > 4	3 ≤ score ≤ 4	1 < score < 3	score ≤ 1
Interacting with teammates	score > 4	3 ≤ score ≤ 4	1 < score < 3	score ≤ 1
Keeping the team on track	score > 4	3 ≤ score ≤ 4	1 < score < 3	score ≤ 1
Expecting quality	score > 4	3 ≤ score ≤ 4	1 < score < 3	score ≤ 1
Having related knowledge, skills, and abilities	score > 4	3 ≤ score ≤ 4	1 < score < 3	score ≤ 1

Teamwork dimension	E	M	R*	S
Contributing to the team's work	≥ 4	3-4	1-2	0
Interacting with teammates	≥ 4	3-4	1-2	0
Keeping the team on track	≥ 4	3-4	1-2	0
Expecting quality	≥ 4	3-4	1-2	0
Having related knowledge, skills, and abilities	≥ 4	3-4	1-2	0

Experiences and insights of the lecturer
Eric Mazur

The reason for using the assessment method

There are a number of reasons why I chose this assessment system. Most importantly, I want to educate persistent problem-solvers who have a desire for understanding and not only for grades. I want students to be confident (in the right doses!) and have a growth mindset. To achieve this, it was necessary to create a culture that encourages creativity and calculated risk-taking – one that takes the stigma out of failure. Failures are the unavoidable price of success. However, for many students failure means they quit and don't keep trying until they understand. It means a lack of confidence in their ability. Students need to learn that failure is only a problem if it is an endpoint. On the way to finding a solution, failure can be very productive as it can teach a lot (what doesn't work, what might work, and what students want to explore in greater detail) and leads to success. I wanted to make failure a learning tool. We designed the assessment system in such a way that students have ample room for errors without compromising their eventual success or grade. Only then can we guarantee that students' learning will be maximized and that they will learn to feel comfortable with the (productive) failures that go hand-in-hand with creativity.

Reflections on the assessment method

I have come to believe that even our best students sometimes fail and the dropouts succeed in the workplace because our assessment is not authentic. Assessment is part of a "hidden curriculum", and an important driver of students' study habits. We need to rethink our approach to assessment to bring about meaningful change in education.

Advantages and disadvantages

This assessment system reflects what students accomplish by the end of the semester, not simply what they accomplish during a specific assignment or exam. The advantage that students immediately experience with this system is that they are relieved from the pressure of high-stakes, cumulative exams, which permits them to focus on their learning. Since the system completely forgives retakes, students can learn from their mistakes and build upon them without having those mistakes affect their grade.

> **Key advice**
> My key advice to teachers is to ask themselves what their role is in the classroom. Why spend time giving a lecture about information that can easily be found online? Instead, repurpose the valuable time spent with students on activities that add value to a mere transfer of readily available information.

Further readings

https://www.insidehighered.com/views/2016/01/19/new-ways-grade-more-effectively-essay

Nilson, L.B., & Stanny, C.J. (2014). Specifications Grading: Restoring Rigor, Motivating Students, and Saving Faculty Time (Reprint edition). Stylus Publishing.

Specifications grading with the EMRF rubric by Robert Talbert http://rtalbert.org/specs-grading-emrf

https://info.catme.org/features/catme-five-dimensions/

8 Evaluation of the golden principles of collaboration

Interdisciplinary skills:	collaboration reflection
Characteristics:	authentic assessment assessment of group work self-regulated learning
Role:	self-assessment
Purpose:	of learning as learning
Course:	Supporting Learning @ the Workplace
Program:	MSc in Learning and Development in Organisations
Institute:	Maastricht University (NL)
Study load:	182 hours
Group size:	30 - 60 students
Year:	first-year master's students
Lecturers:	Wendy Nuis and Mien Segers

More than ever, graduates are expected to collaborate with colleagues. However, examples of for-credit courses in which students get coaching on the process of teamwork are hard to find. The lecturers of this course developed a form of assessment *as* learning by inviting students to reflect individually on the team cooperation and to discuss the results of these reflections collectively with their student team. The team members choose their own focus on what is important for good teamwork. This course is aimed at graduates in the master's program in Learning and Development in Organisations, but the assessment format can easily be adapted to students in other fields of study.

About the course and assessment

Brief description of the course

The master's program in Learning and Development in Organisations challenges students to find ways to support learning and development in an international business environment. The program combines elements from economics, business,

human resource management, and learning sciences. The central questions in the course *Supporting Learning @ the Workplace* are:
- How do you organize learning and development as strategic tools in an organization?
- What are the challenges when (re-)designing, implementing, and evaluating new programs or tools?
- How do organizations make professional learning a strategic tool?
- In the course, students work in teams on a real problem or question from organizations outside of academia. The students act as consultancy teams. The teams have to define and analyze the given problem and come up with a solution resulting in a report and presentation for the client.

Intended learning outcomes that are assessed in this example

The student is able to:
- manage a project in a professional way while making use of the team's resources and diversity and cooperating with the client in a professional way

Collaboration is only a small part of the intended learning outcomes but does receive attention in the master's program as a whole. In a parallel module, students are coached in the skills they want to further develop before graduation, and for some students, the course in this description offers the opportunity to explicitly train collaboration.

Description of the assessment

Working on a project implies working well together as a team. The quality of the result is dependent on the effort of the different team members as well as on their interaction. This means that students need to share knowledge and stand up for their own point of view while also respecting the point of view of others. Another important aspect that facilitates effective teamwork is the creation of a safe atmosphere in which students respect each other, listen to each other, and deal with conflicts in a constructive manner.

All the work that students do in this course is team-based. The teams consist of approximately six team members and are put together by the lecturers, who take into account the different characters and qualities of the students, their disciplinary background, and their preference for a client. In this way, the teams are well-balanced and multidisciplinary.

Teams get a grade for the results of the project and not for the collaboration process itself. Adequate teamwork is a key condition for delivering a good result for the client, and therefore the teams are supported in their evaluation and strengthening of their cooperation. This is done by inviting the students to reflect individually on the team collaboration and to discuss the results of these reflections collectively. The team members choose their own focus on what is important for good teamwork. They formulate five 'golden principles' that contain the team's idea of good collaboration. These principles could, for example, be 'open communication in the group', 'providing feedback to each other in a constructive manner', or 'keeping promises, being honest and responsible'. Three times during the course, the students fill in an online questionnaire and score how good they think their team is scoring on their own golden principles. The report is a reflection/feedback instrument; it is oriented towards helping the development of the group as a team instead of judging the current state of affairs.

On a week-by-week basis, the following steps are taken to make the conversations on teamwork possible and worthwhile.

Week 1 / step 1	The teams formulate the five 'golden principles' they believe are necessary for successful team cooperation. This is based on an extensive introduction session in which the teams get to know each other, discuss their individual qualities, and focus on team-building activities. At the end, they collectively decide and define their five golden principles.
Week 2 / step 2	Each team member is asked to reflect individually on the golden principles via an online questionnaire with the following question: • To what extent is the team working according to these 'principles'?
Week 3 / step 3	The team reflects on the team cooperation. Input for this meeting is the anonymized report from the questionnaire. Of the five golden principles, those that have large standard deviations or a high or low mean score are used as input for the meeting. • Are all principles relevant? • What critical events happened that might have caused negative tension in the team? • How did you deal with it as a team? • What positive flow did you experience as a team? • What evoked this? • To what extent do you feel your team reflects on the team cooperation during the project work? As a result, the team can decide to reformulate the golden principles and collectively decide on the next step to take regarding team cooperation.
Week 5 / step 4	The team fills out the questionnaire for the second time, again followed by a collective team reflection meeting focusing on the five golden principles.
Week 8 / step 5	After the closure of the project and the presentation to the client, the final individual online reflection is sent to the team. The summary of the team results on the golden principles is shared and discussed in the team during the debriefing session. The debriefing session aims to determine the project's successes and to identify the lessons learned with respect to the content of the project, the project management, and the team cooperation. Therefore, it focuses on: • Understanding the feedback received on the project deliverables and formulating lessons learned for the future • Deepening the understanding of how the team interaction has evolved over time

Assessment materials

This is a sample of the questionnaire each team member has to fill in. The five golden principles are examples from one of the teams.

Golden principles of this team	Strongly disagree	Disagree	Neutral	Agree	Strongly agree
1 Open communication within the group, which entails clear discussion about availability and the active involvement of everyone. We provide feedback to each other in a constructive manner.	☐	☐	☐	☐	☐
2 Meetings with structured planning. Equal task distribution and clarity on what should be prepared. If we need help, we will not be afraid to reach out to each other.	☐	☐	☐	☐	☐
3 Efficient teamwork, including writing protocol with what was talked about in the meetings and a summary. Before starting our individual work, we decide together on an outline. In addition, everybody has to be prepared, and what is expected of each person is clearly communicated.	☐	☐	☐	☐	☐
4 Keep promises; be honest and responsible. When work is divided and a deadline has been set, then we commit ourselves to keeping the deadlines and the responsibilities we have as team members. If we have challenges and weaknesses or if we make mistakes, we will be honest about it.	☐	☐	☐	☐	☐
5 Keep a nice and fun work atmosphere, one in which we respect each other and take breaks.	☐	☐	☐	☐	☐

Experiences and insights of the lecturer
Wendy Nuis

The reason for using the assessment method

Although students often work in groups during their studies and are graded on products made by a team, we noticed that they rarely get coaching on the process of teamwork. In this multidisciplinary course, we think coaching the teams helps students to better reach the intended learning outcomes. The five golden principles the teams must formulate help them to feel a sense of ownership with regard to the collaboration in their team. Because the rules are not imposed by the teacher, the students feel more involved and responsible for their own team process, as they have set this as important conditions for a successful collaboration.

Reflections on the assessment method

The team process is not graded but formatively evaluated by the teams themselves. We decided to use a system by which the students evaluate the functioning of the team as a whole as opposed to the team members evaluating each other. This strengthens the sense of collaboration as a common team goal.

Advantages and disadvantages

The focus on the process is an advantage. The coaching on the collaboration is an integral part of the course. If you notice as a lecturer that something is going wrong in a team collaboration, you can intervene in a timely manner, and you have the five principles to base the conversation on. Teams can then discuss how to improve the team collaboration themselves. A disadvantage is that coaching the teams takes quite a bit of time. Reaching all intended learning outcomes is as important as it is in other courses, and coaching the team process adds another layer to the course. New lecturers/coaches would also need to get a feel for how to have meaningful conversations to help the teams improve their way of working together.

Perspective of the student

I felt that this was a unique way of working together in a team. It was hard sometimes but mainly nice and fun. Formulating the five golden principles was not difficult for our team, and this made it easy to address each other on things that weren't going smoothly. The fixed moments with the coach were helpful. The course was very engaging.

> **Key advice**
> Make clear at the very start that team collaboration is essential and that the goals can only be reached by working together. Identify the critical moments during the project or course, and choose wisely when to monitor and coach the team collaboration.

9 Reflection on teamwork and disciplinary expert roles

Interdisciplinary skills:	collaboration reflection
Characteristics:	authentic assessment
Role:	teacher-led assessment
Purpose:	of learning
Course:	From Idea to Prototype
Program:	minor in High Tech, Human Touch: Science to Society
Institute:	University Twente (NL)
Study load:	420 hours
Group size:	48 students
Year:	third-year bachelor's students
Lecturer:	Kostas Nizamis

Prototyping is a common practice in engineering education. But even outside this domain, developing a prototype offers a good opportunity for developing integration, collaboration, and reflection skills. This is especially the case when students from various disciplinary backgrounds develop a prototype in a collaborative effort. In this example, students reflect individually on their role in an interdisciplinary team. The format is applicable to many courses and projects where students need to collaborate in teams.

About the course and assessment

Brief description of the course

The minor *Science to Society* consists of two courses: *From Idea to Prototype* and *From Prototype to Society*. Students perform the role of product developers. They work in groups on a scientifically and practically grounded solution to real-life societal challenges in diverse fields like energy, construction, healthcare, learning, and robotics. Creative design ideas and technological innovations – in cooperation with various stakeholders in academia and in industry – are necessary to tackle these challenges. During the course *From Idea to Prototype*, the participating students are introduced to various disciplines and design and development skills. This is done via a number of tutorials, lectures, and workshops. The background knowledge and skills that are gathered allow the students to share a common language and learn from each other. In the meantime, the student groups delve into the state-of-the-art of the science behind the challenge provided by an external partner or research department, and they look for novel ways to apply their knowledge in an extensive yet agile design process. In the past, solutions have included the design of a distribution system, technology for monitoring or coaching, serious game design, or healthcare support. All groups will walk the path from a specific real-life challenge to one or more scientifically and practically grounded prototype(s) for the challenge at hand.

The intended learning outcomes of this course that are addressed in this example

The student is able to:
- collaborate and communicate with multidisciplinary team members and stakeholders
- evaluate and critically reflect on their own contribution to the team based on their disciplinary knowledge and academic skills

Description of the assessment

This course has four assessment methods: a group report (60%), an individual reflection report (10%), and a presentation assessed by experts (20%) and by peers (10%).

Assessment materials

Instructions for the individual reflection report are given below. The student is asked to reflect on the collaboration in a multidisciplinary team and the project management role they performed.

Amount of words: +/-1000

Briefly describe actions you undertook related to the project management role you wanted to perform (for example, your role as coordinator, planner, contact person, etc.).

Briefly describe actions you undertook related to your disciplinary background. What contributions did you have as an expert in your field (psychology, computer sciences, mechanical engineering, applied sciences, civil engineering, etc.)

Reflect on these actions:
- To what extent did your actions contribute to the project and to your project management role?
- From a disciplinary perspective, to what extent did your actions contribute to the project?
- To what extent were you satisfied with your actions, and why?
- To what extent were you able to use your personal strengths?

When describing these actions and consequences, can you filter some essential aspects that contributed and/or blocked your contribution to the project and personal contribution?

Based on the aspects you filtered from your experiences, write an alternative method you would use to have a better effect in the future (for example during the module From Prototype to Society).

Reflection questions:
- What would you do differently in a future project?
- Has working on this project changed your picture of other disciplines in some way?

Please explain with concrete examples (tip: remember the stereotypes that were discussed in the workshop about multidisciplinary teams).

Experiences and insights of the lecturer
Kostas Nizamis

The reason for using the assessment method

Reflection is a very important skill for students who will enter the labor market in a few years' time. It will help them to be able to sell themselves and to recognize their strengths and their weaknesses in a coherent way. Additionally, it will teach them to always take the time to think and reflect on the consequences of their decisions.

Reflections on the assessment method

Some students have had much more experience with writing a reflection report than others. If I were to teach this course again, I would develop a more hands-on workshop for the students on how to write a reflection report. And I would introduce the possibility of submitting a preliminary report halfway through the course so that students can receive feedback midway. In this way, they would be more prepared for the final report. Furthermore, I would try to enrich the assessment with more elements. For example, I would add how they would grade the effort of each other, or I would have a tutor guiding such a process. And after adding these elements, I would also raising the weight that this reflection has in the final grade. Currently its weight (10%) is too low, as students can ignore it and still receive as high as a nine for a final grade.

Advantages and disadvantages

The main disadvantage we have noticed is that students are more comfortable writing reflection reports if they have had prior experience doing so. For example, psychology students already undergo this process a couple of times and therefore know how to do it, while mechanical engineering students have difficulty meeting the standards. Although technical and engineering students do much of the programming, building, assembling, and so on, they fail to express this in a coherent way. This imbalance is the main disadvantage we have noticed so far.

> **Key advice**
> When designing a new course, have a look at your intended outcomes and think carefully about whether this assessment method is most suitable for the assessment of your objectives.

10 A moot court to build critical thinking skills

Interdisciplinary skills:	integration critical thinking reflection
Characteristics:	authentic assessment assessment of group work
Role:	peer assessment
Purpose:	for learning of learning
Course:	Chain of Evidence
Program:	MSc in Forensic Science
Institute:	University of Amsterdam (NL)
Study load:	168 hours
Group size:	30 students
Year:	first-year master's students
Lecturer:	Maarten Blom

By using a mock crime scene and a moot court, students are put in a real-life situation that they will encounter in their professional life as a forensic scientist. During moot court, students put into practice all the knowledge and skills they have developed during their studies. Using a moot court is an authentic learning and assessment strategy, and arguing your case demands high levels of critical thinking, and communication.

About the course and assessment

Brief description of the course

Students from the master's program in Forensic Science receive exhibits that potentially contain scientific and physical evidence coming from a mock (simulated) crime scene. After pre-assessment of the case, the students design an examination strategy and perform the trace recovery in the laboratory in teams of four to five students. After the traces are secured, they are sent to the forensic lab for analysis. Once the results are received, the students interpret these and write a report or 'expert' opinion. The course concludes with a moot court session during which the students are questioned about the scientific evidence and their report. All students are expected to contribute to the examination of the evidence, the writing of the expert report, and the preparation of the team for moot court.

The intended learning outcomes of this course that are addressed in this example

The student is able to:
- critically establish an examination strategy according to its value given the scenarios
- interpret and communicate the results of the examination of the scientific evidence within the framework of the criminal justice system
- create a case file to record all critical steps and decisions in compliance with guidelines and best practices within the framework of the criminal justice system
- create written reports (forensic report) and formulate verbal statements (moot court interview) to record and communicate the results and interpretation of the scientific evidence of a mock case

Description of the assessment

The case file of the mock crime and moot court are the core of this course. Each team will receive information about the case in the form of an investigation request. In the beginning, the students will be guided through the selection and securing of the evidence and some presumptive/confirmatory testing. Then they will be involved in reporting the results within the framework of the criminal justice system. There will be two written testimonies: one for biological traces and one for the other type of traces.

At the end of the course, after the delivery of the written testimonies, the teams will have to defend their expert opinion in a moot court session with a prosecutor, a defense lawyer, a judge, and a counter-expert. These roles are played by professionals from the field (e.g. judges, lawyers, and forensic experts) and staff members. Although the students are part of their research group, they will answer these questions individually and are allowed to take some time to formulate their answers. Some important aspects in this moot court session include good argumentation for every decision-making step, reference to the quality system used, recognition of possible fallacies, anticipation of the reaction of the defense lawyer or the counter-expert, and one's behavior in the court. The students must also convince the court of the reliability of the methods they used. The nature of the assessment is very open. Anything can be asked.

A week before the final moot court takes place, the teams have the opportunity to practice in the same setting with the judge and other roles represented by the main instructor and forensic experts present. The students are welcome to observe each other's moot court sessions in order to get a feel for what is expected in the final moot court and can give feedback. The teams may improve their reports based on the feedback received.

Critical thinking

Whether it is reasoning what is possible evidence in the mock crime scene, evaluating the weight of the evidence, or preparing for the possible argumentation of the counter-expert in moot court, the students need to apply their critical thinking skills to come to a good result. There are several known fallacies in argumentation that are particular to the forensic field that students need to be aware of and – if not substantiated well – will have a negative effect on the grade of the course. An example of such a fallacy is making inferences on the likelihood of a hypothesis that depends not only on the experts' findings but also on evidence outside the scope of their expertise. Forensic experts should convey the likelihood of their findings given a set of hypotheses that are relevant to both the prosecution and the defense. The data students gather in the first stage of the investigation do not speak for themselves but have to be carefully interpreted. The presence of a counter-expert in the moot court increases the importance of precise argumentation.

Grading

While the grade consists of four elements – a written exam (30%), the moot court report (30%), the final moot court defense (30%), and a little creative assignment (10%) – only the written exam is individually graded. The grade assigned for the moot court defense is the result of the discussions among all the members of the court and at least one of the main instructors. The numerical grade given by the instructor will be equally weighted with that given by peer review (student team) and self-assessment (member of that team), but the grade given by peers cannot be higher than that of the instructor (e.g. instructor = 6, peer review = 6, self-assessment = 4, average = 5.3).

Assessment materials

The focus of this example is on the moot court defense, one of the building blocks for the lecturer to get an idea of the depth that the student groups reached in their analysis.

The moot court **defense** is assessed based on the following criteria:

Assessment form for moot court defense	
Contributing to the team's work	
Argumentation	The student uses valid scientific argumentation to underpin the content.
Critical thinking	The student reflects critically on the strengths and limitations of the accomplished work and provides original recommendations for future research.
Forensic relevance	The forensic relevance is clearly explained.
Target audience	The content of the presentation is adjusted to the correct target audience.

Interaction	
Interaction with audience	The student interacts with the audience when needed.
Interaction in discussion	During the discussion, the student answers the questions correctly and on a sufficient scientific and forensic level.

Experiences and insights of the lecturer
Maarten Blom

The reason for using the assessment method

By using a mock crime scene and a moot court, students are put in a real-life situation that they will encounter in their professional life as a forensic scientist.

Reflections on the assessment method

The moot court is authentic and therefore the most powerful element of the course. This course is one of the last courses of the master's program, and it is an invaluable experience for students to have a glimpse of the concrete professional tasks they will soon be encountering in their jobs.

Advantages and disadvantages

The big advantage of the setup of the course is that it inspires critical thinking, teamwork, and a synthesis of the knowledge that was gained earlier in the program in a very realistic setting. One of the disadvantages is that the amount of group work is quite substantial. This may, therefore, sometimes require extra attention on the part of the lecturer.

The student perspective

The course has a real-life feel because we had to take a professional role in analyzing the crime scene and defending our conclusions in the moot court. As a team, we were thrown in at the deep end and had to operate rather independently. This was something I really liked. We learned a lot and the whole experience felt authentic and fun as well. We as a research team had to contact the police (the lecturer) for info or the prosecutor (again, the lecturer) to give tentative results.

> **Key advice**
> Make sure to really challenge the students with problems that are as realistic as possible - including the fact that most interesting problems have many solutions, each of them are imperfect in some sense. Allow for some trial and error for the students to discover and deal with this.

11 Authentic assessment, learning by accident

Interdisciplinary skills:	integration critical thinking
Characteristics:	authentic assessment assessment of group work
Role:	teacher-led assessment
Purpose:	of learning
Course:	Forensic Engineering
Program:	MSc in Aerospace Engineering
Institute:	Delft University of Technology (NL)
Study load:	168 hours
Group size:	40-50 students
Year:	first-year master's students
Lecturer:	Michiel Schuurman

For this course, the lectures created a simulation of an aircraft accident on campus. Students work in interdisciplinary teams of six to eight students to get acquainted with the industry practice of working in teams, and as a result they experience how valuable it is to work in an interdisciplinary team to solve a complex problem. With this authentic assessment, theory and practice are brought together and students can approach real-world cases and industry practice in the safe environment of the university.

About the course and assessment

Brief description of the course

In the course *Forensic Engineering*, students are introduced to forensic principles used in air safety investigations in a real-life and problem-based learning environment. Another goal is to teach students to appreciate the variety of knowledge and specialism required in this type of inquiry. The course consists of eight lectures, six practical sessions, and an overarching challenge to prepare students for the final practical exam consisting of a simulation of an aircraft accident on campus. The lectures focus on technical and safety-oriented aspects of each phase of an aircraft accident investigation: the fact-finding phase, the analysis phase, and the reporting phase. Since accidents often involve people (pilots, witnesses, or other people), students are also taught about 'living' sources of information during the theory lectures and learn how to interview these sources in the practical sessions. The practical sessions are intended to apply the principles learned during the theoretical lectures – through examples of incidents and accidents with aircraft – to highlight different (technical) failure modes and characteristics, to stimulate critical thinking, and to teach students the required skills and teamwork. In the practical sessions, students work in interdisciplinary teams of six to eight students to get acquainted with the industry practice of working in teams and to learn how to follow multiple lines of research concurrently. The students were shown examples of accidents that at first glance seemed 'easy' to solve. Only if students use a non-biased research approach with fact-based observations they can come to a substantiated conclusion. During practical sessions, students are given limited information about the event and are instructed to analyze the accident and determine the likely cause (or causes). The diversity of the accident scenarios requires students to apply a wide variety of disciplines ranging from aerodynamics structures and flight performance, and students are therefore divided into groups with different 'experts' based on their specialization track. At the end of each practical session, each group reports to the class on that topic about what happened and why it happened. During this discussion, students learn that the technical background influences the students' hypotheses, judgment, and conclusions. In this way, students experience how valuable it is to work in an interdisciplinary team and learn that this can even be necessary to solve a complex problem.

The intended learning outcomes of this course that are addressed in this example

The student is able to:
- apply investigative principles used in air safety investigations
- describe and analyze findings and formulate recommendations for improvements
- discuss design principles and knowledge deficiencies from cases

Description of the assessment

The final exam is an investigation of a simulated accident outside on the grounds of the university and carried out in the same student teams as in the practical session. The exam consists of two parts: field investigation (50% of the final grade) and a final report (50% of the final grade). The field exam starts with a short briefing, and then the teams have an hour to examine the accident site. Three lecturers are present, but they are not allowed to answer questions or comment on what happened. They are only there to assist students as needed and to assess each group based on a predefined set of observation and grading criteria. Then students have two weeks to write a report with facts, analyses, and conclusions, including the formulation of recommendations to prevent reoccurrence or to mitigate the consequence of future events.

Assessment materials
Assessment form

Assessment criteria	Feedback
Field Investigation • Factual observation and scene documentation • Interview (for example with eyewitnesses and pilots) • Organization, communication, and decision-making of the team	
Report • Content/grammar • Factual detail (what observed) • Factual reliability (how formulated) • Analyses of soundness (how formulated) • Analyses of hypothesis (reasoning) • Conclusion • Recommendation	

Experiences and insights of the lecturer
Michiel Schuurman

The reason for using the assessment method

We wanted to teach students that reality is not like television, and we wanted to challenge students' misconceptions about accident investigation, influenced by news shows and 'documentaries' on various television channels. We wanted to let students experience the real world because, after all, you train students to work in the real world. The goal was to bring theory and practice together and to approach the real world in the safe environment of the university.

Reflections on the assessment method

We have noticed that this form of assessment makes students more motivated and involved in their studies. We often get the question from students whether they can contribute to the course next year, for example by registering as witnesses who can be interviewed by students during the exam. In addition, we have noticed that some students are startled when they first enter the simulated accident site and are put out of their comfort zone. During the lectures and practical sessions, they have learned how to search for facts and conduct interviews and yet they are sometimes not fully prepared for reality. They become stressed due to the one-hour time constraint and the overwhelming amount of information present on the site. We take this into account by keeping a close eye on the students.

Advantages and disadvantages

The advantage of this assessment form is that students learn to work together and are better prepared for the real world. Students also appreciate this in this course and experience it as a confidence builder. Despite not knowing what to expect, they are not afraid to tackle it and appreciate the challenge. The disadvantage is that it is a lot of work for the teacher to organize, coordinate, and come up with something different every year. Yet this also makes it challenging for us to come up with something even more creative than last year.

Key advice
Give your course some time to develop and mature. You have to experience what works and what doesn't, and this takes time. Involve students from the previous years because they know better what students face than the teacher. Feedback from previous years' students will contribute to making the course and assessment better.

Further reading

Saunders, G., Schuurman, M., & Rans, C. (2016, September 12-15). Teaching Forensic Engineering Teaching Students Critical Thinking by Investigative mindset [Workshop]. 44th SEFI Conference, Tampere, Finland. http://resolver.tudelft.nl/uuid:1402a506-c044-4155-8f98-2ab46af16502

12 Grading the contributions to class discussions

Interdisciplinary skills: integration   critical thinking

Characteristics: authentic assessment

Role: teacher-led assessment

Purpose: of learning

Course: Introduction to migration studies

Program: minor Global Migration

Institute: University of Amsterdam (NL)

Study load: 336 hours

Group size: 50 students

Year: second-year bachelor's students

Lecturer: Hein de Haas

In this example, students are assessed on their ability to develop a comprehensive and critical understanding and on their active participation in class discussion. By grading students' participation, the lecturer hopes to trigger the intrinsic motivation of students and that it helps to bring classroom discussion to a higher level. The grading criteria can be used in courses in other fields which have the aim of developing students' ability to contribute to discussions on complex societal problems.

About the course and assessment

Brief description of the course

The course *Introduction to migration studies* offers students a comprehensive and critical understanding of migration processes and enables them to make a critical, independent assessment of media information and political discourses. In the course, various 'migration myths' and misleading 'push-pull' models are challenged. Students analyze migration as an intrinsic part of larger processes of development and social transformation in destination and origin societies rather than as a 'problem to be solved'.

To achieve this, students discuss theories on the causes and continuation of migration, the role of states and policies in shaping migration patterns, experiences of settlement, incorporation, and integration in destination societies as well as the social, cultural, and economic consequences of migration for origin societies. The diversity of impacts and experiences of migration are highlighted by reviewing migration experiences in all world regions. This will help students to achieve a global perspective on migration, going beyond common Eurocentric views that frame migration as essentially being about journeys from poor countries in the global south to the wealthy global north. The participation grade is connected to a weekly assignment in which students prepare critical questions based on the literature they read that week. The course takes 16 weeks, and students hand in 11 weekly assignments.

The intended learning outcomes of this course that are addressed in this example

The student is able to:
- criticize common ways of categorizing, framing, and analyzing migration
- criticize scientific, media, and political discourses on migration and migrants and dissect their underlying assumptions
- combine insights from different disciplines to understand and analyze migration-related social phenomena

Description of the assessment

Students are encouraged to contribute to class discussion with preparatory weekly assignments wherein they formulate critical questions regarding the weekly texts. Because the lecturer is convinced that academics need to be able to intervene in discussions and come up with critical questions and new perspectives, student participation in class is key. Class participation provides students with the opportunity to practice speaking and persuasive skills as well as the ability to listen.

Assessment materials

Fifteen percent of the course grade will depend on contributions to the class sessions. The lecturers of the seminars keep track of the intensity and quality of individual participation. The class participation is assessed on a scale of 1-10. The grading criteria is given in the scheme below.

Outstanding contributor (grade 10)	Contributions in class reflect exceptional preparation. Ideas offered are always substantive and provide one or more major insights as well as direction for the class. Challenges are well-substantiated and persuasively presented. If this person were not a member of the class, the quality of discussion would be diminished markedly.
Good contributor (grade 8)	Contributions in class reflect thorough preparation. Ideas offered are usually substantive and provide good insights and sometimes direction for the class. Challenges are well-substantiated and often persuasive. If this person were not a member of the class, the quality of discussion would be diminished.
Adequate contributor (grade 6)	Contributions in class reflect satisfactory preparation. Ideas offered are sometimes substantive and provide generally useful insights but seldom offer a new direction for the discussion. Challenges are sometimes presented, fairly well-substantiated, and are sometimes persuasive. If this person were not a member of the class, the quality of discussion would be diminished somewhat.
Non-participant (grade 4)	This person says little or nothing in class. Hence, there is not an adequate basis for evaluation. If this person were not a member of the class, the quality of discussion would not change.
Unsatisfactory contributor (grade 2)	Contributions in class reflect inadequate preparation. Ideas offered are seldom substantive and provide few if any insights and never a constructive direction for the class. Integrative comments and effective challenges are absent.
Students who **never** participate receive 1 point for participation.	

Students will be informed about their current standing halfway through the course as well as at the end of the course.

Experiences and insights of the lecturer
Hein de Haas

The reason for using the assessment method
With this method, the students are well-prepared for the seminar and the group discussion. By grading their weekly assignments and their class participation, students' intrinsic motivation – their inner drive – is triggered. They learn to formulate their thoughts. The connection with the weekly assignment is important because students need prompts before being able to participate in a discussion. This allows the level of the discussions in the classroom to thrive and reach a higher level.

Reflections on the assessment method
For some students, participating in group discussions is very difficult because they have trouble formulating their own thoughts and coming up with critical questions. Some students have already learned to participate in discussions at home while growing up, while others need more practice. During weekly office hours, students can come by to discuss their progress and can receive feedback on how to improve their weekly assignments and participation.

Advantages and disadvantages
The advantages are that students are prepared for class, and their preparation and participation are rewarded. This improves the atmosphere during seminars since students are motivated to participate. A disadvantage is that it is a lot of work for the lecturer to read and grade the weekly assignments.

> **Key advice**
> To avoid misunderstanding, I advise lecturers to be very clear about the criteria for the different grades. Make clear what you expect from students and specify when they are an adequate contributor or an excellent contributor.

13 Dance assessment as experiential learning

Interdisciplinary skills:	critical thinking reflection
Characteristics:	assessment with rubrics
Role:	teacher-led assessment
Purpose:	of learning
Course:	Integrative seminar 4: Societal Challenges. Bridging self and other through mind and dance
Program:	BSc in Politics, Psychology, Law and Economics
Institute:	University of Amsterdam (NL)
Study load:	168 hours
Group size:	16 students
Year:	second-year bachelor's students
Lecturer:	Lela Mosemghvdlishvili

In this experimental course, dance improvisation is used as a prime assessment tool to allow students to gain a deeper understanding of concepts as empathy, compassion, and consciousness. By doing this, students are able to obtain knowledge through direct observation and experience within their own body. The lecturer experienced how movement practice can be integrated in the learning process and can nurture students' soft skills as well as create novel ways to facilitate deep thinking and reflection. This is perhaps not a form of assessment that is easy to apply in every context, but it is a challenging and innovative example.

About the course and assessment

Brief description of the course

In this integrative seminar, students are invited to consider and reflect on the role of academia in responding to societal challenges and their own possibilities of action and responsibilities as interdisciplinary researchers. Students will be stimulated in critical and reflective thinking, collaboration and experiential learning, which means learning through experiencing and doing. The emphasis is put on nurturing students' soft skills such as the ability to reflect and be self-reflexive, to explore, to acknowledge and appreciate personal vulnerabilities and strengths, and to appreciate humbleness and develop imagination. Students discuss what it means for a being to be and how we understand one another. In the course, students take time to consider concepts such as mind and consciousness, and empathy and compassion.

The lecturer hopes to create an open space to compel students' deep thinking and engagement with their own emotions, values, and ideas. In this way, students are encouraged to observe and reflect on their own understanding of self. Additionally, they explore possibilities as well as limitations of empathizing with, relating to, and understanding each other. Students' skills such as the ability to listen, empathize, and relate to each other's emotional states are most valued in this course.

Alongside traditional classroom settings such as readings and discussions, students will have an opportunity to explore analytical concepts through body movement and dance. Various techniques and exercises from modern, folk, and circle dances will be used to help students overcome constraints (shyness), bond with each other, allow creative self-expression, and most importantly enable the deep integration of knowledge through movement in a safe and non-intimidating environment.

The intended learning outcomes of this course that are addressed in this example
The student is able to:
- contribute creatively to analyze the problems and come up with innovative solutions, which requires the integration of knowledge
- develop soft skills, specifically empathetic capacity

Description of the assessment
Along with keeping a reflective journal (60%) and participating in class discussions (20%), students express subjective experiences in a mediated dance form (20%). As an end product, students get together in pairs to create a short performance, where they choreograph a chosen concept without words and music through movement in space. The assignment is to create a choreographic piece (one to three minutes) on a selected analytical concept that was covered in the course content (e.g. alienation, empathy). The activity involves students researching the concept through movement, creating abstraction, memorizing the sequence of movements, rehearsing, and performing it. During the process, the lecturer and peers give feedback on the 'raw' dance. Students receive a grade for this assignment.

Assessment materials
Grades for the dance performance are determined by a grading rubric that focuses on the following categories: **clarity of purpose** regarding which concept is being abstracted and performed through dance; **creativity and unique delivery** of the content; and **movement invention**.

Poor	Fair	Good	Excellent
Clarity of purpose (30%)			
Audience members find it hard to discern the purpose (analytical concept) that is expressed through the choreography. The choreography appears disconnected from the topics/key concepts covered in the course.	The central purpose is somewhat visible in the choreography but not fully maintained throughout the whole performance.	The central key concept that has been abstracted is clear and the choreography is staged in a way that makes identification of the concept by the audience easy.	The central key concept of the choreography is evident and easily identified by audience. It is sustained throughout the whole performance.
Creativity: Unique delivery (30%)			
Did not successfully deliver content. Choreography is unable to hold audience interest or express the content through body movement in space.	Choreography is somewhat literal and resorts to direct illustration/enactment of the concept.	Choreography demonstrates the team's own interpretation of the key concept. Uses a variety of expression forms to deliver the communicative intent to the audience.	Project demonstrated students' unique interpretation and expression of the selected key concept. It is performed with a variety of dance expression forms in an excellent manner.
Movement invention (20%)			
Team demonstrates a poor skill level in movement invention in response to a selected concept.	Team demonstrates an adequate skill level in spontaneous movement invention in response to a chosen concept.	Team demonstrates a variety of movement invention by using different tools for dance expression (rhythm, repetition, accent).	Team demonstrates an excellent skill level in creating new and interesting movements. In designing the new movements, the coordination between dancers creates a unique choreography between the dancers.
Performance skills (20%)			
Team members demonstrated confusion on the stage. Choreography was not memorized. Dancers showed little engagement. Lacked coordination.	Team members demonstrated knowledge of individual parts, but attunement with each other can be developed and improved.	Choreography was well performed. There was no evidence of confusion on the stage. Each participant has memorized and correctly performed own part in the choreography. Demonstrated enthusiasm during the performance through facial and body expressions.	Demonstrated full immersion in choreography by well-coordinated movements and appropriate facial and body expressions. Each team member was in attunement with rhythm and tempo of the group choreography. Individual parts were memorized, clearly articulated, and skillfully performed.

Experiences and insights of the lecturer
Lela Mosemghvdlishvili

The reason for using the assessment method

Dance as a learning activity and assessment form originated from the idea of learning through direct experience. A concept of knowledge (*paññā* in Pāli) used in Buddhism inspired the development of this part of the course. Three types of knowledge are distinguished. The first is learned knowledge or borrowed wisdom (*suta-maya-paññā*) that comes from reading books and listening to teachers; the second is reflective knowledge (*cinta-maya-paññā*) that is acquired through pondering and logically thinking about what one has learned. The third is superior wisdom (*bhāvanā-maya-paññā*) and can be viewed as experiential wisdom, which means obtaining knowledge through direct observation of meditative experiences within one's own body (Thēpwisutthimēthi, 2017). Training students' empathy through dance and body movement is a form of experiential learning. Dance is one way to elicit experiential learning through their body.

Reflections on the assessment method

What I learned is that it is possible to assess in a non-traditional manner, although I felt personally insecure. In the first year that I taught the course, I implemented dance in my course but did not grade it. In the second year, it was a pass/fail assessment. By the third year, it was graded in more detail. It comes with experience over the years to get acquainted with and confident in assessing in a non-traditional way. The second thing I learned is that by adjusting the traditional classroom setting – for example, mingling as a university teacher between the students – you can create a burst of trust and openness. In next year's course, I would like to document the dance performances better.

I am thinking of video-recording the performances so that they can be preserved. It is like a positive memory we can keep. We can look back and see what it means to receive a certain grade. In this way, the performances can also be shared with the next cohort.

Advantages and disadvantages

Dance can create opportunities for critical thinking in the classroom. During the process of making the dance or performance, students incorporate and integrate literature and practice sound decision-making. In that sense, it strongly resembles more usual assignments that students undertake such as writing an essay or giving an oral presentation. Besides, dance can greatly enhance trust and openness and create a safe space in the classroom. Dancing and body awareness can be a supplementary tool to engage students better, to help them experience and reflect their own learning process, and to improve the group dynamic.

The biggest advantage is the enthusiasm of students. I think nothing is more rewarding for a lecturer than seeing your students coming into your classroom with a smile – a clear sign that they want to be there. I experienced it as a very pleasant and rewarding learning atmosphere and drew a lot of energy and inspiration from how enthusiastic the group was.

The student perspective

For me, this course was rewarding not just academically but even more so personally because it let me reassess how I was approaching academia and made me reflect on what knowledge is. The course required me to be open and vulnerable and it helped me deal with stress. The dance assessment itself was a learning experience. With dancing, you are less in your head and it has elements of fun. It also helps me to bond with classmates. Normally every working group is similar, you kind of know what to expect. Dancing with your classmates is something completely different from sitting with them in a classroom. It results in the active participation of everyone in the room. A disadvantage is that not every student feels comfortable in the beginning. Therefore, I think it is important to make an effort to include everyone. There needs to be safety mechanisms in place.

> **Key advice**
> Using dance or body movement as an assessment form may seem difficult, but in practice this can be done anywhere. You don't need a dance studio; with a little effort, you can enact physical movement in any classroom. Be open to this possibility. Do not be scared to ask your students to get up in the classroom.

Further readings

https://experiential-dance.com/teaching/

Thēpwisutthimēthi, P. (2017). *Under the Bodhi Tree: Buddha's original vision of dependent co-arising.* (B. Santikaro, ed.). Somerville, MA: Wisdom Publications.

McGarry, L.M., & Russo, F.A. (2011). Mirroring in dance/movement therapy: Potential mechanisms behind empathy enhancement. *The Arts in Psychotherapy, 38*(3), 178-184.

14 Enhancing critical thinking with Perusall

Interdisciplinary skills:	critical thinking
Characteristics:	self-regulated learning
Role:	peer assessment
Purpose:	for learning · as learning
Course:	Pathophysiology and Neuropharmacology
Program:	BSc in Psychobiology
Institute:	University of Amsterdam (NL)
Study load:	336 hours
Group size:	100 students
Year:	third-year bachelor's students
Lecturer:	Erwin van Vliet

In this example, the lecturer makes use of a platform that helps students to reflect on their difficulties when reading and understanding texts. Students receive and give feedback and learn from each other. By observing and mimicking peers, students learn to be critical thinkers.

About the course and assessment

Brief description of the course

Pathophysiology and Neuropharmacology is a third-year elective course for students of the bachelor's program in Psychobiology. In this course, knowledge from the fields of pharmacology, genetics, molecular cell biology, pathophysiology, psychiatry, and neurology is integrated at all levels: from the molecule to the human mind. This integration takes place by considering how brain functions can be disrupted and how this can lead to various brain disorders, and by looking deeply into the pharmacokinetic and pharmacodynamic aspects of drugs involved in these disorders. Interactive lectures are given by experts in the field in which the latest developments in research are discussed. There are flipped classroom tutorials in which students work on the study material in a team-based manner. At the end of the course, students give a presentation about a pathophysiology of their choice and possible pharmacotherapies to treat or cure this disease.

The intended learning outcomes of this course that are addressed in this example
The student is able to:
- provide a summary of common pharmacotherapies and explain how they lead to relief of clinical symptoms
- identify the different aspects of the research & development of medicines and explain how they are applied in the development of new medicines
- evaluate the problems associated with the use of the available neuropharmaceuticals and how new drugs could be developed as a result

Description of the assessment
This course uses Perusall, a free, online social learning platform to promote pre-class reading compliance, engagement, and conceptual understanding developed by Eric Mazur at Harvard University (see example 7). In this course, Perusall is used both as a teaching method for practicing critically reading of a scientific article and as a method for assessing critical thinking.

Perusall for assessment for learning
The first step is to ask students to collaboratively annotate a scientific article. Students start a new annotation thread in Perusall by highlighting the text, asking a question, or posting a comment. In this way, students can indicate what they find unclear in an article and thus can receive feedback on where they stand. As a second step, students react to each other and resolve each other's questions by giving a reply or comment to an existing thread, like in a chat with one or more students. So students receive and give feedback since they receive quick answers to their questions by peers, help others resolve their questions, and learn from each other. And as a last form of formative assessment, students are asked to 'upvote' the answers to their questions that they like best. Experience shows that high-quality 'critical thinking' questions about the article and answers to these questions are upvoted by students. In this way, students receive feedback on their critical thinking skills or get examples of high-quality 'critical thinking' questions asked by their peers.

Perusall for assessment of learning
Perusall is also used as a summative assessment of critical thinking skills by counting as 2% of a student's final grade of the average of four assignments. In this case, the lecturer rates the extent to which a student is offering informative questions or comments, helping their peers address their questions or confusion, and stimulating discussion via their annotations. The rating is recorded in a grade book in Perusall.

Assessment materials
Lecturers can adopt the suggestion for a grade given by Perusall that is based on automatic annotations that include the following for each student: when, how often, with what comments (based on text analysis), and distribution over the text.

Experiences and insights of the lecturer
Erwin van Vliet

The reason for using the assessment method
The main reason I started using Perusall is that I want students to practice reading scientific articles critically. I was looking for a way to get students to come to lectures prepared and to give them insight into the main and side aspects of articles by reading it critically. I sometimes notice that students do not read or understand preparatory articles because they do not ask high-quality critical questions during lectures. I think this is a missed opportunity for students and guest lecturers because it prevents them from having a scientific discussion about the article. It is precisely this discussion that ensures that students learn a lot and at the same time makes teaching more fun.

Reflections on the assessment method
The reason I am so pleased with this assessment method is that it enhances social learning in a very natural way. Students give each other feedback, ask each other questions, can upvote those questions, and interact with each other about the content.

Advantages and disadvantages
In my opinion, Perusall has many advantages for both students and lecturers. Lecturers can integrate the articles into the study material much more easily. And on the basis of the confusion report, you can easily find out what students understand and what they are having difficulty with. Now, after years of teaching, I find out that my students do not understand certain topics so I have subsequently adapted my teaching accordingly. The assessment about the articles have been made well this year. The assessment method fulfilled my aim of getting the students to read articles more critically, even if the summative assessment grade is only 2% of the final grade. This low percentage of 2% is based on experiences with Perusall at the University of Groningen and on the advice of Eric Mazur. Students experience it as a reward that they do receive a grade for it but at the same time are not stressed about it because it does not feel like a tough assessment.

There are in my opinion no real disadvantages to this method. Students indicate that Perusall takes a lot of time, but that's exactly the point. It just takes time to critically read an article. It also forces students to spread out their work in studying the material and to procrastinate less, so I actually think this is an advantage.

> **Key advice**
> Think carefully about why you want to use Perusall. It is not a trick; it needs to have a purpose and it must fit with the constructive alignment of the course. There are also a number of conditions that must be met in order to use Perusall successfully. For example, it is important to have a good infrastructure. In our case, the copyright goes through the library and we have a coordinator who knows how it works and who can help lecturers who have practical questions. This helps to lower the threshold for lecturers to get started.

Further readings

Miller, K., Lukoff, B., King, G., & Mazur, E. (2018). Use of a Social Annotation Platform for Pre-Class Reading Assignments in a Flipped Introductory Physics Class. Frontiers in Education, 3.

King Gary: An Introduction to Perusall (https://gking.harvard.edu/files/gking/files/ph.pdf)

https://perusall.com/

15 Co-creation of a rubric to encourage ownership of learning

Interdisciplinary skills:	reflection
Characteristics:	authentic assessment assessment with rubrics assessment of group work
Roles:	self-assessment peer assessment teacher-led assessment
Purpose:	for learning of learning as learning
Course:	Developing Learning Cultures in Organizations
Program:	BSc in Child Development and Education
Institute:	University of Amsterdam (NL)
Study load:	252 hours
Group size:	30 students
Year:	third-year bachelor's students
Lecturer:	Frank Cornelissen

This example showcases how assessment and feedback can be used to promote the development of self-regulated learning. Self-regulated learning refers to the active control by students of some aspects of their own learning: for example, the setting of learning goals and the monitoring and regulating of progress towards the attainment of these goals. This is an example of an assessment practice in which students develop a grading rubric to encourage them to take ownership of their own learning.

About the course and assessment

Brief description of the course

This course, part of the bachelor's degree in Child Development and Education, focuses on an understanding of the way strong learning cultures can be developed in organizations. With the guidance and feedback of lecturers, students work together in small consultancy teams (two to four persons) on authentic questions from a variety of public and private organizations. Besides the content-related learning outcomes of the course, students develop an ability to combine consultancy and research skills for problem-solving in an authentic context, to formulate and substantiate their own view, to weigh the views of others, and to be open and critical towards their own view and those of others. The course revolves around four consecutive phases of the consultancy process: (1) acquisition, (2) analysis, (3) advice, and (4) report. The assignment consists of preparing their advice for the client, presenting this advice at the university, and writing an individual reflection essay on theory and practice.

The course is designed from the perspective of collegial pedagogy in which university teachers and students are partners in learning and mutually dependent on each other's skills and perspectives to generate quality work. Students and lecturers meet in weekly sessions that resemble the work of a consultancy firm fostering an open and free exchange of ideas. The center of attention moves away from the lecturer so that everyone becomes a member of a community of learners.

The intended learning outcomes of this course that are addressed in this example

The student is able to:
- guide their learning process towards their own learning goals
- collaboratively work with a client as well as with peers

Description of the assessment

In Week 5 of this eight-week course, students develop a grading rubric as a group. This grading rubric is used both during the final oral group presentation at the university and for the assessment of the individual, written reflection. Developing a grading rubric encourages students to take ownership of their own learning because it allows students to reflect on quality markers of their own work as opposed to relying solely on their lecturer's judgment of the work. The rubric (see example below) includes the criteria for success and briefly describes the three different levels of quality.

During the group presentation, students give peer feedback as formative assessment. Students assess the quality of their fellow students' work and provide one another with feedback using the grading rubric. The teaching team then decides on the final grades on the basis of the rubric.

Assessment materials

Example of the grading rubric for presentation to the client as developed by the student teams.

Objectives	Open for improvement	Adequate	Excellent
1 Understanding the organization The team can outline the current learning culture of the organization. *The team conveys its understanding of what is happening in the organization.* **Feedback** Score, description of observed behavior, strengths, suggestions for improvement	• The team gives a vague overview of the specific organization. • The team does not show a comprehensive knowledge of the learning culture of their organization. • The team does not address their client's focus and/or goal(s).	• The team provides a clear outline and description of the specific organization. • The team gives a good description of what kind of learning culture the organization has. • The team gives a good description of why a learning culture within the specific organization is important. • The team explains their client's focus and/or goal(s) in a coherent and understandable manner.	• The team gives an in-depth outline of how the specific organization functions and how functions are related to each other. • The team shows a deeper understanding of the learning culture and provides several points of views to support their understanding. • The team shows a more deepened insight into their client's focus and/or goal(s) and explains why these focus/goal(s) are of value to the organization's learning culture.
2 Applying proper methodology/ theory The team demonstrates (explains) their use of methodology and theory behind their advice and/or analysis. *The team can combine consultancy and research skills for problem-solving in an authentic situation.* **Feedback** Score, description of observed behavior, strengths, suggestions for improvement	• The team did not think about their methodology. • The team does not use any theory to back up their advice.	• The team explains which methodologies they used and why they did so as well as why they did not use other obvious methodologies. • The team shows that they used some theories from literature.	• The team can justify in depth which methodologies they used and why they used them. • The team correctly provides practical solutions and sufficiently supports their ideas with literature evidence.

3 Presentation of advice The team can provide the client with insight into their own situation and the pathways for improvement.	• The team has difficulties in presenting the advice in a clear, understandable way. • The team does not have visual or literal material to back up their presentation. • The team does not present improvements coherent with the presented problem. • The team does not provide insight into their client's situation, has a shallow explanation, and/or no examples.	• The team's advice fits partly with the problem presented. • The advice is well thought out but not clearly presented. • The pathways of improvement are apparent but lack innovation and creativity. • Insight into client's situation is clear and presented, but without examples.	• The advice fits the problem presented. • The advice is well thought out and clear. • The next stages are made apparent (practical or abstract/process-based). • The advice is creative, using both theory and original, innovative thought. • Insight into their client's situation is clear, and supported by examples from observations.
Feedback Score, description of observed behavior, strengths, suggestions for improvement			
4 Professional presentation performance Good preparation from the team, engagement with the chosen client, enthusiastic, good structure and flow, constructive/clear/informative slides.	• There is little cohesion between the material presented and the team. • The team seemed unprepared for the presentation. • The team could not hold the audience's attention. • The team was not able to manage their time well for the presentation. • The team was not prepared for the client's questions and could not respond to their questions. • The team showed no enthusiasm at all for the project. • The team did not establish eye contact with the audience.	• The team was prepared for the final presentation. • The presentation was easy to follow. • The team held the audience's attention but without engaging them. • The team was able to respond to the majority of the client's questions. • The team showed interest in the project but no enthusiasm. • One of the members of the team did not establish eye contact with the audience. • The body language of the team was active but did not use hand gestures.	• The team was prepared for the final presentation and included creative material. • The presentation was easy to follow (good flow and logic). • The team was able to hold the audience's attention and engaged with them throughout the presentation. • The team had good time management. • The team was able to respond to the client's questions. • The team showed enthusiasm and interest about the project. • The team established eye contact with the audience.

	• The body language of the team was tense and didn't seem confident. • The members of the team were reading the slides.	• The slides were only a visual aid and the team sometimes read from them.	• The team's body movements were active and used hand and face gestures. • The team did not simply read the presentation slides.
Feedback Score, description of observed behavior, strengths, suggestions for improvement			

Experiences and insights of the lecturer
Frank Cornelissen

The reason for using the assessment method

We promote self-regulated learning by arranging a supportive learning environment that enables students to practice self-regulation. It is for this reason that we have opted for a collegial pedagogy, with one of the key characteristics of the course being that the students and lecturers all become members of a community of learners. The assessment of the course is aligned with these principles. Students take part in the assessment process themselves, enacting collaborative assessment.

Reflections on the assessment method

I see great benefits in involving students in the assessment because checking one's progress against clearly defined and well-understood criteria promotes learning and self-regulation. When done well, collaborative assessment offers benefits for both students and lecturers.

Advantages and disadvantages

Almost all students valued the assessment process in the course. It proved once again that students can give very good feedback to each other based on a grading rubric. Furthermore, this feedback does not differ from what we as lecturers would have given. The advantage of peer feedback based on a self-developed grading rubric is that students also learn to self-evaluate their own work as a result of applying assessment criteria to the work of their fellow students. An added practical benefit is that there is simply more feedback that students can receive from peers than we as university teachers could ever provide on our own.

For the university teacher team, it is important to recognize that students need sufficient time to revise and improve their work on the basis of feedback from their peers and lecturers. This year the feedback was given during the final oral presentation to the client, and since this occasion was the last meeting, students were unable to adjust their presentation as a result of the feedback. Next year we would make the formative aspect of the assessment stronger by bringing the feedback to the fore during a test presentation. I also want to make an earlier start with the development of the rubric.

> **Key advice**
> When practicing collegial pedagogy, it is crucial for lecturers and students to have equal status. For example, involving students in defining the assessment criteria fits well in this didactical approach.

16 Peer and self-assessment for student-led activities

Interdisciplinary skills:	collaboration reflection
Characteristics:	authentic assessment assessment of group work self-regulated learning
Roles:	self-assessment peer assessment
Purpose:	of learning as learning
Course:	Education Development and Social Justice
Program:	MSc in International Development Studies
Institute:	University of Amsterdam (NL)
Study load:	168 hours
Group size:	25 students
Year:	first-year master's students
Lecturer:	Mieke Lopes Cardozo

If your aim is to develop your students as agents of change, then this will have consequences for what and how you teach. The lecturer in this example developed a learning strategy according to her pedagogical beliefs. The students in the course co-create their own learning activities and are (partly) responsible for their own and their peers' assessment. This allows students to have agency over their learning progress.

About the course and assessment

Brief description of the course

Starting from a critical theoretical and historical perspective, students in this course critically assess the past and present global governance of education processes and both dominant and counter-hegemonic policy repertoires. Students explore a critical view on educational change – and education as a mechanism for potential societal change – as a complex relation between macro-level policies and micro-level policy translations into practices, influenced by historical and larger socio-economic, socio-cultural, and political transformations. Using co-creation, teachers and students introduce and analyze key theoretical lenses, main concepts, and current debates and controversies in the field of education and development from a transdisciplinary, relational, gender-aware, and multi-scalar perspective while paying specific attention to non-hegemonic and decolonizing theories and resources. Students are encouraged to take an active part in co-creating this collective learning space, making joint decisions on relevant case studies and contributions. Together, teachers and students learn about the reproductive and transformative power of education and examine educational change as a process of convergence, struggle, and debate about aims, curriculum, knowledge, methodologies, and practices. Students develop their own positionality in these debates, enhancing their debating and negotiation skills and networking opportunities through interaction and dialogue with practitioners and policymakers in the field. The course design is inspired by the lecturer's engagement with regenerative development and living systems thinking (Regenesis, 2020).

The intended learning outcomes of this course that are addressed in this example
The student is able to:
- critically reflect on their own educational trajectory (prior to and throughout this course) and assess their (individual and group) contributions to the co-created learning space in this course

Description of the assessment
The assessment of this course consists of three parts.

Activity	Open for improvement	Counts for	Role
Group roleplay	Each student participates in a group roleplay	40% of final grade	teacher-led assessment
Student-led learning activity	Each student chooses to contribute to *one* group student-led activity • a student-led studio (creative and engaging exercises connected to key readings/themes), or • the design and facilitation of the roleplay	30% of final grade	self-assessment peer assessment
Individual reflection document	Each student creates an individual assessment and reflection essay to reflect on their own learning, the process and outcomes of the group work, and the transformative potential they see for education	30% of final grade	self-assessment teacher-led assessment

As an individual exercise for this course, students are invited to develop a reflection document in which they assess their own learning as well as the process of teamwork in the groups. This exercise is meant to allow students to reflect on:
- their personal purpose for joining this course and how they organize their own learning;
- the quality of their contributions (both individual and group) to the co-created learning progress of the group;
- the process of their own learning trajectory (prior to this course and within this course).

Students are asked to provide a suggested grade range for the roleplay (group grade), the student-led activity (group grade), and the self-assessment reflections (individual grade). The suggestions are taken into consideration by the lecturer when grading the work.

Assessment materials

Students use the task cycle and guidelines for peer assessment and self-assessment of the student-led activities.

The task cycle (based on Regenesis, 2020)

This task cycle can help you to *design* your group-led activity (the studio, the design of the roleplay, or any other task you are working on such as your essay or planning an important meeting). You are encouraged to use this task cycle to reflect on the process of design and implementation and to evaluate the process and outcomes afterwards.

As a team, start by defining the collective purpose of your task by formulating it in the following way:
- To… (describing the task),
- In a way that… (this reflects the benefit of the process to the group),
- So that… (this reflects the benefit of the outcome for the group, the broader field, and any other specific audience).

Then consciously formulate the desired product (what will be produced?), followed by the process (what methods and means are needed to accomplish the product?), and the functioning capabilities (what knowledge, skills, material, and resources are needed?). Be as specific as possible.

Peer and self-assessment guidelines

Students use the task cycle exercise above to reflect on their own learning and the process of group work. They are free to use it in a (creative) way that makes sense to them. Based on their reflections, they are invited to indicate a grade range for the activity that they were involved in as well as for their own reflection exercise. This suggestion is taken into account by the lecturer when doing the final grading.

Form 1: peer and self-assessment for the student-led studio or design team for roleplay, and the final roleplay

Your name:

Group members' names for student-led activity:

Group members' names for roleplay:

Reflections on the learning as part of group work in two teams
- What was your team's collective purpose for the student-led activity? (To… so that… in a way that…)
- What was the desired outcome of your group work? What methods and means did you work on to support this desired outcome?
- What was your unique contribution to the learning process? How did you relate to others in their learning process and contributions?
- What was most challenging in the teamwork, and how did you (yourself or collectively) resolve this?
- What did you appreciate most about the teamwork in these two teams?

Suggested grade range for your group
(student-led studio or design team of the roleplay):

Suggested grade range for your roleplay team:

Form 2: Self-assessment of your learning during the course

In your reflection here, please consider the following questions:
- What was *your* purpose for joining this course? (To... so that... in a way that...)
- Reflect on your key motivations for joining this course. How do you experience this sense of motivation/drive now?
- What key capabilities did you aim to develop, and how much of your aims have you reached?
- How did you feel about your own learning process when you started the course, and what has shifted in you throughout the duration of this course?
- What do you aim to work on moving forwards?

No suggested grade needed here, but you are encouraged to express in one word how you would characterize your own learning during the course.

Form 3: Reflection essay on your understanding of the transformative potential of education for development and social justice, drawing on resources and reflections from the course

In this part of the individual exercise, you are invited to reflect more deeply on the contents of the course and how these had an impact on your understanding of the transformative potential of education in terms of addressing social injustices or fostering equity, inclusive development, and diversity. Make sure to refer to at least five of the required resources we worked with in this course. You are free to bring in additional (academic or non-academic) relevant resources to support your reflections:

Intended grade range *for this course* at the start of this course	*Please indicate the grade you intended for this course at the start (see first survey) and, if you wish, any reflections on this retrospectively.*
Suggested grade range *for this peer/self-assessment and reflection essay*	*Please indicate here the grade range for this entire document (steps 1, 2, and 3). Please note that this will count for 30% of the final grade.*

Experiences and insights of the lecturer
Mieke Lopes Cardozo

The reason for using the assessment method

Based on the research and teaching I have done over the years, I have come to realize the transformative power of education but also the fact that most education systems and the cultures and structures we are in do not always allow for that potential to take place. My drive behind experimenting at first and now further refining and exploring these alternative forms of teaching and assessment is really to allow student agency to become something more meaningful: to step away from assessment forms that are very technical and standardized and measure certain skills and to widen the view of what university education can bring. If our program claims to develop agents of change later on with our graduates, then how do we actually do that through our education?

The topic of this course is very suited for this type of unique assessment because we study education as a source of social justice and transformation. For me, this has been a path – and will be a path for many years to come – to try to explore how to walk the talk, that is, not just reading about social justice and education for transformation or the negative impact education may also have in reproducing inequalities, for example. So it is walking the talk and stumbling upon obstacles and failing as we go along and having the courage to feel vulnerable as a lecturer. I try to make this transparent as well, especially with the roleplay. If the roleplay design team doesn't do their work, then no one in the course has a final assessment moment. It could completely collapse, actually. Of course, I have a backup plan because I have done roleplay for many years and I can roll out one of my roleplays and let people do that, but it wouldn't be the same. I think we should dive into the deep end with everyone, and it is that shared responsibility that makes a difference and builds agency.

Reflections on the assessment method

I always try to take the comments from the students from that year and use that in the redesign of the course together with a student that is assisting me in the course. There is always a student voice from the start that can help me to translate the feedback from the previous year in the course manual and hold me accountable. For me, it's important to keep in mind the learning objectives: what is it that this course wants to create, and how do we balance the different aspects?

Advantages and disadvantages

One of the benefits is that grading is a lot more fun and more engaging. The disadvantage is that it takes time, because I also write short personal reflections for each student. It is a challenge of the overall course, and I reflected on this in class. This course used to be 12, then 10, then 9, and now 6 Eurepean Credits. Because it's such short timing, it is quite hard to do full justice to this process of reflection and feedback. Also, some students stated that they appreciated the feedback on the studios, but I wasn't able yet to give individual feedback to everyone.

The student perspective

For me personally, the course is incredibly engaging, it's something you can get really passionate about, you can get really into this roleplay. I also appreciate the freedom and the fact that students are encouraged to showcase what they're good at. In the studios or the roleplay, if you're good at public talking that is great, but maybe you're good at designing group activities or group work. Formal assessment can be discouraging for people if you're not good at something and everybody is looking at you.

I understand the decision for student-led studios and roleplay but both of them being group grades, there're always some problems or disadvantages for group work. I personally like to work in groups, but sometimes I want to completely do my own thing and own my product.

The self-assessment was very challenging, because I can be really hard on myself. It was a bit weird for me to grade myself. I talked to classmates and they were all struggling with suggesting a grade. Everybody wants to suggest a good grade because the lecturer is going to take that into account. But did you actually do that well? And how can you know how you did? It is just being very self-reflective and honest about how you participated in class. I think it is nice, but being self-reflective is also difficult.

Key advice
- Make students co-responsible for learning activities and assessment. Trust that it will bring out the best in them and that you can let go of what happens in the classroom. Rely on your skills and experiences as a teacher to improvise and to just be there.
- It takes more time for the lecturer to do co-creation, but the key here is preparation. Make sure there is enough time to prepare and to engage students in the process even before the first class starts.

Further reading
Regenesis: Institute for Regenerative Practice. (2020). https://regenerat.es

17 From feed-up to feed-forward

Interdisciplinary skills: reflection

Characteristics: self-regulated learning

Roles: self-assessment peer assessment teacher-led assessment

Purpose: for learning as learning

Course: Experimentation year 2

Program: BSc in Psychobiology

Institute: University of Amsterdam (NL)

Study load: 420 hours

Group size: 200 students

Year: second-year bachelor's students

Lecturer: Sandra Cornelisse

Reflecting thoroughly on academic skills can be challenging. The lecturers in a series of interrelated courses developed rubrics to help students to assess their skills themselves and to become independent and self-directed learners. In these courses, students receive and give feedback, learn to process this, and are able to convert this into concrete follow-up steps.

About the course and assessment

Brief description of the course

The course *Experimentation year 2* consists of a series of five interrelated sub-courses spread out over the whole second year. The sub-courses focus on research skills, problem-solving, collaboration, and critical thinking as well as receiving feedback and processing it themselves. Students work on experiments on a project basis and conduct increasingly independent research by formulating research questions, creating research designs, analyzing results, and discussing. They present their projects with a research report or scientific presentation. The five sub-courses are

assessed separately but in conjunction with each other on the basis of an overall rubric for the second year for the components:
1. practical work,
2. academic attitude,
3. presentation, and
4. report.

The rubrics of the practical component are aligned with each other. For example, in the rubric for the report, the weighting of the criterion *discussion and conclusion* increases towards the end of the year: at the start of the year, 20% of the assessment is based on the conclusion and discussion, and towards the end of the year this weight is raised to 30%. The rubrics provide feed-up for the students at the beginning and feedback during the course. By using the same rubric in several sub-courses, students know beforehand what is expected of them. They have more insight into the assessment criteria and can reflect more profoundly on them. The rubrics are aligned with the development of skills during the program and makes the feedback more powerful.

The intended learning outcomes of this course that are addressed in this example

The student is able to:
- give and process feedback
- reflect on his/her own work and actions and adjust this if desired

Description of the assessment

At the end of each sub-course, students formulate their feed-forward with regard to the four rubrics for the components:
1. practical work,
2. academic attitude,
3. presentation, and
4. report.

Feed-forward means providing students with information that leads to greater learning possibilities, for example enabling self-regulation over the learning process by offering strategies to do so. Feed-forward has a powerful impact on learning and closes the gap between where students are and where they aim to be, giving them ownership of their learning process. You ask students to reflect on where they should go next.

Assessment materials

Halfway through the course as well as at the end, students are asked to use the criteria in the rubrics for a self-assessment (feedback) and to write a short self-evaluation based on the following questions:

Top	Tip
What do you think is your strongest point (based on the rubric criteria) and why? What are you going to do to maintain this?	What did you find most difficult and why? How do you want to improve this?

Some students write these evaluations at the task level, while others focus more on the process level. A minority of students relate to their own learning process and describe which steps they want to take to keep growing. Below are some examples of student self-evaluations.

Top	Tip
I think my strongest point is cooperation. I can consult well, give my opinion clearly, but leave room for others. If I notice that someone is saying less, I try to involve them in this so that all opinions are listened to.	*What I found difficult is asking critical questions and participating in a scientific discussion. I want to improve this by reading more about the relevant topic that the discussion is about and perhaps asking questions more actively.*
One of my strongest points is that I can take a critical look at my own work and draw appropriate conclusions / points for improvement. I think on both of these points, I don't have to do much to keep it. Because it comes naturally, I have to make sure that I keep practicing this. There is always room for improvement!	*I sometimes find it difficult, although I appreciate feedback, to show it in a concrete way in a follow-up step. I can improve this by focusing even better on what is expected of me so that I can better place the feedback in the process.*

> *I find the strongest point of my academic attitude is to actively participate in the lesson by asking questions and entering into conversations. Because of this, I always have the feeling that I have gained more information at the end of a workgroup or collaboration. So I try to keep pushing myself to ask questions and to start discussions, even though I sometimes find this exciting because I am afraid to say the wrong things. Pushing myself outside my comfort zone ultimately helps in the development of my knowledge and skills.*

> *I find the most difficult point of the academic attitude is to deviate from my established working method in the field of organizing. I always like to work through my own planning because in my opinion this works best for me. It is important for me to improve this because I myself tend not to really spread things out but to do things in one go, so that the knowledge does not have time to sit in your head and be processed. I'm going to try to improve this by really sticking to the prescribed schedule (being active in Perusall well in advance).*

At the same time, lecturers provide feedback to the students per rubric. Students are asked to compare their own completed rubric with that filled in by the lecturer. In the first working group of the next sub-course, the feedback of the self-assessment and the lecturer's feedback are discussed and compared with each other under the supervision of a university teacher. To enhance self-directed learning, the following questions are discussed:

- Which feedback of the self-assessment or lecturer is of importance to you?
- Which feedback do you take as a starting point to develop?
- How do you want to tackle this?
- Which feedback has been addressed in the previous sub-course?
- Did you achieve your development goals?

This feedback and feed-forward cycle will be repeated in consecutive courses until the end of the academic year. This also gives students a better insight into how they have grown in the past year, allowing them to use it in the next academic year if desired.

Experiences and insights of the lecturer
Sandra Cornelisse

The reason for using the assessment method

We noticed that students did not always take the feedback from previous assignments into follow-up assignments that build on this. This is unfortunate, especially since it is valuable information that can help students to improve themselves. The different sub-courses are also often supervised by other university teachers, which makes it difficult for the lecturer to keep an eye on the student's learning trajectory. By paying attention to the questions described, the student learns to process and reflect feedback on a self-directed basis, and the lecturer can provide feedback that is in line with the improvement points of the students and is also included in follow-up assignments.

Reflections on the assessment method

I always design my courses according to constructive alignment and also coordinate the moments and ways of feedback so that students can take the next step in their learning process in as self-directed a manner as possible to achieve their learning objectives. I have noticed that students sometimes find self-direction and feedback processing difficult, depending on student motivation and how useful they experience it. It can help students to experience that if they process the feedback they receive, the next similar assignment they have will be better. One obstacle to allowing students to experience this is that courses often stand on their own and are closed, and thus there is not always a clear continuous line that lecturers and students are aware of. Also, lecturers need to communicative effectively with each other about what happens in previous and subsequent courses to be able to give and process optimal feedback.

Advantages and disadvantages

One advantage of this method is that students learn in a self-directed manner to process feedback and to improve not only their current assignment but also follow-up assignments. In addition, they learn to place the current assignment in line with what they have learned before and what follows and thus can learn more purposefully. Furthermore, integration of feed-forward from a previous course takes relatively little time because students discuss the feed-forward at the beginning of each practical in their group.

A disadvantage is that there are a number of preconditions for a continuous feedback and feed-forward cycle to work. First of all, the rubrics and assignments must be aligned. Secondly, students must be guided in answering the questions, preferably during a working group or practical so that they know each other's development points within their group and can support each other in this. Finally, it is only applicable when it comes to skills and attitude.

> **Key advice**
> Use the continuous feedback and feed-forward cycle together with the teacher team as widely as possible within successive subjects or parts of the study program. To be able to use it successfully it is essential that various components and assessments are properly coordinated within a curriculum.

18 Comparative judgment as a tool for learning

Interdisciplinary skills: collaboration critical thinking reflection

Characteristics: self-regulated learning

Role: peer assessment

Purpose: for learning as learning

Course:	English proficiency
Program:	BSc in Literature and Linguistics
Institute:	University of Antwerp (BE)
Study load:	84 hours
Group size:	70 students
Year:	second-year bachelor's students
Lecturers:	Alena Anishchanka and Jennifer Thewissen

Peer feedback is in itself a powerful tool for learning, but in this example the strength of peer feedback is paired with the strength of working with comparison. If students compare texts and give each other feedback, they build up their sense of the criteria of the rubric and what quality work looks like. This also makes them think about their own texts and how others read their essays.

About the course and assessment

Brief description of the course

The course *English proficiency* is an integrated skills course for speaking, listening, reading, and writing for second-year bachelor's students in Literature and Linguistics. Students expand their advanced English lexicon and practice to verbally formulate complex and nuanced opinions on topics related to everyday life and current affairs. The focus is on the terminology related to English-speaking countries both in the cultural and political field. The students improve their writing skills in a number of fixed genres like formulating a clear research question, related arguments, and a logical introduction and conclusion.

The intended learning outcomes of this course that are addressed in this example

The student is able to:
- effectively and fluently contribute to discussions within and outside their own field of study while making use of abstract notions and expressions
- show understanding at a reasonable speed and with a critical mind general and academically specific texts
- prepare and conceptualise texts within their domain of study as well as outside, make notes or write an essay which bears witness to good communication skills
- give fellow students feedback on their written texts

Description of the assessment

In this course, students peer-review each other's written work and give comments. This is done by using a specific software tool called *Comproved* (earlier called DPAC). This software was developed at the University of Antwerp and uses the power of comparison and ranking in the way students assess each other's written pieces or other student work. The students write short essays and then get assigned ten essays from fellow students that they have to read and compare. This step is repeated three times throughout the course, so the students have to compare 15 sets of two essays. Each time, the topic of the essay is different but the process is the same. The essays are allocated randomly and anonymously by the Comproved tool. The students compare the essays in terms of the overall quality of the work and additionally have to comment on their peers' work. The students are given the criteria for quality in the form of a rubric but can compare and evaluate the essays holistically; they don't have to give feedback on each specific aspect in the rubric. Once all the students have compared the texts assigned to them, the software calculates the ranking of all the essays in one overview. This is done anonymously. By seeing how their texts are ranked and looking at the notes of their fellow students, the students get a feeling of what quality looks like in English writing, and they understand how to improve their own work to meet the criteria.

After the ranking of the students' work, the lecturer discusses the results and the feedback they gave each other with the whole group and asks the students why they think the highest-ranking essay is high-quality work. Together with the lecturer, the students then reverse-engineer this by looking at the criteria for good essays. This discussion makes it possible for students to internalize the criteria, to know how to give useful comments on a text, to know what is expected of them, and to understand how to interpret the comments of their peers and how to improve their writing.

The software is used more than once during the course so that the students get a feeling of how the tool works. The feedback is not graded and is used purely to help students learn. At the end of the course, the students hand in one final paper that the lecturer grades. This final paper is a revised version of one of the essays for which the students received feedback. The peer feedback does not play a role in the summative grading of the course and thus is fully formative in nature.

Self-regulation

When students receive feedback, they must select which comments are worth following up on to improve their texts. This also makes them aware of the quality of the comments they give to others. Furthermore, when students give feedback to someone else, they do this with their own work in mind and have an extra chance to see their own text in a new light. All of the processes mentioned are not a result of instruction by the lecturer but are metacognitive processes that give the students more autonomy in their learning. The iterative process of giving and receiving feedback ameliorates students' thinking about which steps to take to improve their texts.

Assessment materials

The tool used is the comparative tool to be found on Comproved.com.

Experiences and insights of the lecturer

Alena Anishchanka and Jennifer Thewissen

The reason for using the assessment method

The choice for using the comparative tool Comproved is partly driven by necessity. In a course with 70 students, it is impossible to give a lot of feedback to all individual students. Future translators or lecturers need to read and correct numerous texts in their professional life, so using this tool is in a way a real-life setting since students need to collaborate and deal with a number of deadlines. The students learn to internalize the criteria, and even if their proficiency in English is not yet at a high level, they are still capable of telling which text is better than another.

Reflections on the assessment method

Some students found it strange to assess the work of peers and didn't feel at ease with the task. In response to this, I explained to them that they are constantly assessing the lecturers of the courses they take – consciously or subconsciously. For some of them, that was a revelation. The essay text that the students selected as the best essay is in our experience indeed the best text. The students are very capable of recognizing quality. At the same time, many students felt that the comments they received from their peers weren't of high quality. The irony is that 80% felt this way. The tool works better with students that are already a bit mature and inclined to see the benefits of getting comments from their peers.

Advantages and disadvantages

The method works for large groups of students and is easy to scale up. The bottleneck is that the comments students give to each other aren't checked for quality. Some students felt that the anonymity of the feedback triggered more negative comments. It is great that you can actually do some meaningful work with large numbers of students. Technically it is a well-researched and good tool, as it does well what it is designed for.

> **Key advice**
> Comparing work via the described tool is very new to students and for teachers too. Explain to your students why you are using this assessment method and take time discussing what good quality feedback is. The tool is more fitting for master's students than first-year students because the former tend to see the benefits of the given peer feedback.

Further reading

Conference paper: Capturing learners' responses to computer-mediated peer-feedback in English Proficiency (https://dial.uclouvain.be/pr/boreal/object/boreal:221299).

19 The co-creation of assessment criteria

Interdisciplinary skills:	reflection
Characteristics:	self-regulated learning
Roles:	self-assessment peer assessment teacher-led assessment
Purpose:	for learning as learning
Course:	Sensors and Sensibility
Program:	ATLAS (Technology and Liberal Arts and Sciences) – University College Twente
Institute:	University of Twente (NL)
Study load:	84 hours
Group size:	8 students
Year:	first- and second-year bachelor students
Lecturers:	Pascal Wilhelm and Jose A. Alvarez Chavez

Self- and peer assessment are important aspects of assessment-for-learning practice. Assessing their own work or that of others can help students to develop their understanding of the learning outcomes and the assessment criteria. In this example, students develop the criteria for assessing their work and their peers' work for a 3-D model.

About the course and assessment

Brief description of the course

Sensor and sensibility is a course for students in the bachelor's program ATLAS (Technology and Liberal Arts and Sciences) who are interested in interdisciplinary research. The course explores the relationships between measurable physical parameters extracted from the human body and the psychological meaning that can be attached to those parameters. The focus is on sensors, which are artificial device that produce a continuous flow of data. These data reflect concurrent changes in internal physical phenomena. The way sensors do their work is based purely on natural science; however, since these internal phenomena are also affected by mental states, the sensor data becomes a way to study human experience. Students investigate how sensors work and how reliable they are. They also study to what extent internal physical/physiological phenomena reflect mental states and how valid sensor data are for exploring human experience. All learning activities take place in small groups of students: literature and empirical research, presentations, peer feedback, and building a 3-D instructional scrapheap model of a sensor. There are four deliverables for this course; the first three are team products, and the last one is individual.

Deliverable 1: Historical account.
This is a 15- to 20-minute group presentation on how a particular sensor came into use in particular research fields.

Deliverable 2: 3-D instructional scrapheap sensor model.
In a group, students build a durable 3-D model from disposable materials that demonstrates a sensor concept.

Deliverable 3: Brief research report.
In a group, the students set up, execute, and report a small-scale experimental study for which data from at least one type of sensor is used.

Deliverable 4: Individual reflection and self-evaluation.

The intended learning outcomes of this course that are addressed in this example

The student is able to:
- explain the functioning and data output of at least three types of sensors
- describe sensor development in a historical context
- compare and contrast the use of a particular sensor in different academic fields and put this in a historical context
- explain how psychological constructs are operationalized with sensor data
- execute and report on a small-scale experimental research study that uses sensors to study human behavioral responses under controlled conditions
- critically assess the validity and reliability of sensor data for research on human behavior

Description of the assessment

The unique and innovative aspects of this assessment are the way in which it is established and the major role that students play in it. The assessment consists of three steps:
1. the co-creation of assessment criteria,
2. peer assessment and assessment by lecturers and experts, and finally
3. self-evaluation.

Step 1: Co-creation of assessment criteria

For each of the four deliverables, students take the lead in deciding the criteria on how to assess whether the intended learning outcomes of the course are being met. During a group session, students are asked to come up with criteria they can use to assess their work. At the end of the session, a list of criteria is handed in and the lecturers will integrate all the criteria in an assessment form, one for each deliverable. The lecturers will guide the students during this process, but the students have the final say in deciding on the criteria.

Step 2: Peer assessment and assessment by lecturers and experts

Students then use the form to provide written feedback on each other's work for each criterion. In addition, students also receive feedback from lecturers and industrial design experts at the University of Twente.

Step 3: Self-evaluation

The feedback is input for each student's written individual reflection and self-evaluation (Deliverable 4). This document, which also contains all the feedback received in an appendix, contains a reflection on what the student learned. It also addresses the question whether the student thinks he/she attained the intended learning goals of the course based on the written feedback. Teachers will justify the self-evaluations and give additional feedback. The justification will include a statement on whether the course is passed or not.

Assessment materials

Below is an example of a completed assessment form for Deliverable 2: the scrapheap sensor model. With this 3-D model from garbage material, which students must present at an exhibition for children, they show in an innovative way whether or not they achieved the learning goals. In the first column of the rubric, the feedback criteria are described and learning goals (LG) that are related to this deliverable are stipulated (e.g. LG1). Students, lecturers, and experts – in this case industrial design experts from the University Twente – provide written feedback in the second column. When finished, they send it as an attachment in an email to the students.

Criteria	Feedback
1a The main functions of the sensors are represented in the model – *concept/idea (LG1)*	*The main function of the sensor (measuring temperature) is not immediately clear, but the working concept is.*
1b The main functions of the sensors are represented in the model – *execution/materialization*	*The working concept (so not the function) is represented in an appealing way, fit for the target group.*
2a The main components of the sensor are represented in the model – *concept/idea (LG1)*	*The main components are there, but still some explanation is needed to recognize them.*
2b The main components of the sensor are represented in the model – *execution/materialization*	*I think the materialization could have been more appealing and clearer in the sense that the audience can understand the context (i.e. can see immediately that it is about measuring temperature).*
3a The model shows the data the sensor produces – *concept/idea (LG1)*	*This was somewhat clear, but I think there might be a conceptual gap between marbles rolling into a box and measuring temperature that was not bridged in the model.*
3b The model shows the data the sensor produces – *execution/materialization*	*A temperature level was indicated on the box, but it was difficult to see how the data are being produced (i.e. the marble rolling – temperature indication connection, but this is difficult to visualize, I think).*
4a The model is self-explanatory and can be understood by and is appropriate for the target group – *concept/idea (LG1)*	*I think the model is not self-explanatory. In its current form, quite some explanation is still needed.*

4b	The model is self-explanatory and can be understood by and is appropriate for the target group - execution/materialization	*I think the main function/concept is materialized well, but the whole context could be represented in a more authentic way (it is easy to see, however, how this can be improved with more budget).*
5	The manual contains two examples of application of the sensor that are relevant for/understandable by the target group (LG3a)	*Examples are there and can presumably be understood by the target group. Will the concept of stress be clear, however? Perhaps better to give examples of highly stressful situations.*
6	The model and manual should explicate how sensor output is used to create meaning / to measure a psychological concept (LG4)	*This is explained, but an example in the manual (see above) might have fostered understanding in this case. From the model, this was not clear.*
	Quality of the model, for example in terms of durability (e.g. resistant to movement and touch), use of disposable materials, appealing-ness, interactivity	*A rugged design of disposable materials. Could be more appealing, but the use of the marbles and table tennis balls is creative, as well as the possibility to manipulate the atoms.*
	Additional feedback (if applicable)	*I think your (interactive) visualization of electrons and atoms colliding etc. is clear, insightful, and engaging.*

Experiences and insights of the lecturer
Pascal Wilhelm

The reason for using the assessment method

The initial reason for this assessment format was the wish to experiment with a more active role for students. We asked ourselves: can we develop a course that predominantly relies on peer feedback? We as a teacher team of the bachelor's program ATLAS wanted to create a contemporary learning environment including innovative assessment.

Reflections on the assessment method

I really enjoyed teaching this course, and students reported having enjoyed it too. I am satisfied with the different types of assessments that are part of the course. The assessment of the 3-D scrapheap model was something new. It is a different, innovative end product to show what has been learned. Students had to make a sensor model from garbage material, which they presented at an exhibition. Students viewed and assessed each other's models, as did experts. This was all feasible since we had a small group of students, but I can imagine this could be a challenge if the group becomes larger.

Advantages and disadvantages

The advantage of self-evaluation and peer assessment is that students realize how hard it is to define proper assessment criteria and provide sufficient feedback for learning. They have to rely on peer feedback and they can see how assessments are being made because the method is very transparent. Students steer their own assessment, and they experience ownership. An additional advantage is that it is very time efficient for the lecturer, since your job is to read the self-assessment and decide whether or not you agree.

A disadvantage is that this type of assessment is mostly suitable for a pass/fail assessment because it is very hard for students to assess each other on different levels of (academic) mastery. But for me the focus is not on having students generate grades but rather providing opportunities for them to be able to identify what constitutes a good piece of work. Also, students have to be competent in giving feedback so that the feedback does not become superficial.

> **Key advice**
> - Prepare your students for the task of giving feedback. When they are being asked to sit in the chair of the assessor, they should be prepared to do the job.
> - Think about alternative assessment types. Be courageous and try out different innovative forms of assessment. If it doesn't work out, that's fine. If we don't try new things, we will all judge in the same way. There are plenty of alternative end products you can think of for authentic assessment that involve students more in their learning process and thus ensure that students learn more.

Further reading

https://www.kuleuven.be/english/education/teaching-tips/feedback/peer-feedback.

20 Reflection on interdisciplinary competences using a portfolio

Interdisciplinary skills:	integration collaboration critical thinking reflection
Characteristics:	portfolio assessment self-regulated learning
Roles:	self-assessment teacher-led assessment
Purpose:	for learning of learning as learning
Course:	cross-curricular
Program:	BA/BSc in Liberal Arts and Sciences
Institute:	Utrecht University (NL)
Study load:	-
Group size:	-
Year:	first-, second-, and third-year students
Lecturer:	Merel van Goch

Reflection is a complex, rigorous, intellectual, and emotional enterprise that takes time to do well (Dewey, 1933). Based on the ideas of Dewey, the bachelor's program in Liberal Arts and Sciences at Utrecht University developed a cross-curricular portfolio assignment to challenge students to reflect from different perspectives on how courses, course elements, and extracurricular activities have contributed to their academic, professional, and personal development with respect to five different roles: the researcher, the specialist, the intellectual, the professional, and the citizen.

About the course and assessment

Brief description of the program

Liberal Arts and Sciences (LAS) is a bachelor's program that offers students the opportunity to research and develop their personal talents and interests and to train them as critical academics with well-developed intellectual and academic competences, a sense of social responsibility, and an interdisciplinary way of thinking. LAS students become 'disciplined interdisciplinarians' through the combination of broad learning (in the program's general education courses), deep learning (in the specialization courses), integrative learning (in the program's core courses), and reflective learning (in the portfolio). In the second year of the program, students start with their specializations. Students can choose from more than 40 specializations such as economics, religious studies, biology, sustainable development, cultural anthropology, and international relations. LAS has a strong focus on self-directed learning and the development of self-authorship.

Description of the assessment

At LAS, a portfolio is used as a reflection tool throughout the entire program. The portfolio must be submitted to the assessing lecturers when applying for the bachelor's exam at the end of the third study year. The bachelor's exam can only take place if the assessment of the portfolio assignment is at least 'sufficient'. A sufficient portfolio contains four reflection essays, an overview of the study plan, the results achieved, written essays, a curriculum vitae, the capstone thesis (and assessment form), the interdisciplinary final group project, and the internship, exchange, or honors report. In each reflection essay, they are invited to think and write about their development with respect to five roles.

Assessment materials

Students are asked to reflect on their academic, professional, and personal development with regard to five different roles.

The researcher	Someone who knows how to formulate relevant research questions, can answer these questions in a scientifically responsible way, and is able to present his or her findings in an adequate manner to a relevant forum.
The intellectual	Someone who has obtained a good level of general and cultural development and has a broad perspective that crosses the borders of his or her own discipline. An intellectual is able to adequately connect insights from different scientific disciplines.
The specialist	Someone who has obtained knowledge, insights, and skills in one discipline. This means, among other things, that this person can evaluate both his/her own work and that of others adequately, responding to the criteria that are common in that scientific discipline.
The professional	Someone who takes responsibility for his or her own performance and development. This means that a professional systematically analyzes his or her own behavior and uses this to set adequate goals and make adequate decisions.
The citizen	Someone who has a clear take on what to do outside academia and professional life. A responsible citizen reflects on his or her place in society (now and in the future).

The portfolio includes four reflection essays written at the end of the first semester, at the end of the second semester, at the end of the third semester, and after semester six (just before their graduation). In the second semester of the first year of study, a tutor meeting is devoted to the rationale of working with the portfolio and writing reflections.

Students are asked to describe what they experience (The What) and to provide an analysis and explain their experience (The How). For example, a student wrote: 'To me, doing interdisciplinary research was as if several glasses (lenses for perceiving reality) were fused together into a kind of 3-D glasses that can better map the complexity of reality.' Only the last assignment in year three is graded as pass or fail. In order to pass, students must score a satisfactory score on at least four of the eight criteria listed in the form below, of which at least twice in the last column (explaining how) and at least once in each role.

Role		Criterion	Describing (what?)	Explaining (how?)
Researcher	1	Evaluates his/her own proceedings regarding research skills related to the process and results of the bachelor's thesis		
	2	Evaluates his/her skills in the field of written and oral reporting of research (results)		
	3	Reflects on own development of thinking and reasoning skills that are necessary for adequate scientific practice and application		
Intellectual	4	Is aware of the ways of thinking in the different disciplinary courses		
	5	Compares and contrasts research fields and methods		
	6	Seeks and discovers/creates substantive relationships between the different courses		
	7	Describes/explains how knowledge from one discipline can be applied in another context		

Specialist	8	Reflects on the scientific developments within the chosen main direction		
	9	Reflects on the conducted research within the main direction		
Professional	10	Reflects on own performance in the field of independent and goal-oriented work		
	11	Reflects on own choices during study and future career		
	12	Reflects on own development of social skills when working on projects in a team context		
	13	Reflects on own development of communication skills when working on projects in a team context		
Citizen	14	Reflects on own place in society (ethical and societal)		
	15	Reflects on future profession in society		

At the end of the first year, the student instruction for the portfolio assignment is as follows.

> As a **researcher**: After your first year, you have gained experience in writing papers (formal writing assignments in which you were asked to meet the scientific criteria). Describe what you think is most important in a scientific paper. Did you notice whether there are different criteria for papers in various disciplines? Do not just describe that you have learned something; clearly state what you have learned and how you learned this. Evaluate your proceedings and add documents that support this – for example, papers.
>
> As a **(future) specialist**: You have chosen a major. How did you make this decision and what do you expect to learn from your major?
>
> As an **intellectual**: Describe – or better yet, explain – how the interdisciplinary courses have contributed to your development as an interdisciplinary thinker. Try to explain how each course contributes to the bigger picture and aim for as few 'loose ends' (courses that are not placed in this bigger whole) as possible.
>
> As a **professional**: In the end terms of the bachelor's degree in Liberal Arts and Sciences, professional attitude is described as 'being able to plan a project and to execute this plan, is able to work in a team, and has the necessary social and communicative skills'. To what extent have the interdisciplinary courses contributed to your development of these skills? (Reminder: describing is good, explaining is better). Did you develop your collaboration skills in other courses too?
>
> The **citizen**: Students and alumni of the bachelor's program in Liberal Arts and Sciences often think about complex societal problems such as sustainability or justice. Is there a specific cause you are committed to? Have you started wondering what you might want to contribute outside academia and professional life?

Experiences and insights of the lecturer
Merel van Goch

The reason for using the assessment method
At LAS, students compile their own program to a large extent. For students, it can be a challenge to connect all the different components of the program. That is why it is crucial in this type of education for students to reflect on their learning and to be helped with self-directed learning. The portfolio is a form of formalizing this and of assessing the self-authorship component.

Reflections on the assessment method

This cross-curricular portfolio is combined with reflection assignments within our core courses where students are asked to reflect on the development of their writing skills, for example, and on interdisciplinarity. In my experience, this combination of reflection assignments within courses and cross-curricular works very well. Some of the just-in-time reflection assignments within courses pertain to ongoing group work and collaboration skills. Cross-curricular assignments ask the student to look back and put their individual development on center stage.

Advantages and disadvantages

The advantage is that students are forced to be explicit about the choices they make. This allows them to get a grip on the study program and on what kind of person they are within and outside of their study. Students become aware of their unique profile, which helps them write motivation letters for jobs or master's programs.

The disadvantage is that most students realize the usefulness of the reflection assignments only at the end of their studies. By the time students graduate, they sometimes judge the reflection reports they made in their first and second years harshly. A further disadvantage is that the first three reflection assignments (in academic year 1 and 2) are not assessed with a pass or fail. This sometimes leads to less motivation for the cross-curricular assignments. We have not yet found a solution for this, because I do believe that grading the first assignments (instead of just providing formative feed-forward) is also not desirable. The first three assignments are essentially exercises that build up to the final reflection portfolio.

> **Key advice**
> A prerequisite for teaching students to reflect on their learning process and metacognitive skills is that you, as a teacher, can and are willing to do this yourself. It's important that all teachers and tutors value reflective practice. My advice is to collectively reflect on your role as teachers and on the purpose of higher education in order to sharpen the vision on teaching that drives the team.

Further readings

Dewey, J. (1933). How we think. Buffalo, NY: Prometheus Books (Original work published 1910).

Rodgers, C. (2002). Defining reflection: Another look at John Dewey and reflective thinking. Teachers college record, 104(4), 842-866.

Van Goch, M.M. & Van der Tuin, I. (2018, February). 'Citizenship' and portfolio use in interdisciplinary liberal education. Poster presented at the National Interdisciplinary Education Conference, Eindhoven.

Van der Lecq, R. (2016). Self-Authorship Characteristics of Learners in the Context of an Interdisciplinary Curriculum: Evidence from Reflections. *Issues in Interdisciplinary Studies, 34*, 79-108.

Final remarks: towards new ways of assessment

With this handbook, we want to inspire you with new ways of thinking by giving you state-of-the-art examples of meaningful assessment methods and guide you to think systematically about the assessment of your interdisciplinary education. It can also provide a foothold when you want to put more emphasis in your education on developing interdisciplinary skills like integration, collaboration, critical thinking, and reflection. The handbook shows how to assess students' ability to cross the knowledge barriers between scientific disciplines and between academy and society or their ability to integrate this knowledge. In this final section, we summarize the lessons learned from the examples in this book and show the next steps that can be taken to make assessment more meaningful.

To identify the lessons learned, we distilled the following key points from the examples in Part 2:
1. more emphasis on assessment *for* and *as* learning,
2. powerful feedback,
3. alignment of assessment with the intended learning outcomes and assignments,
4. alignment of assessment with your pedagogical beliefs, and
5. authentic assessment tasks.

We would stress that all these elements are interrelated and that assessment in general needs basic prerequisites such as transparency, validity, and reliability.

Lessons learned for meaningful assessment in interdisciplinary education

More emphasis on assessment *for* and *as* learning

One of the main messages of this book is that in order to make assessment meaningful, there should be more emphasis on assessment *for* and *as* learning. There is a noticeable imbalance between the purposes of assessment, with too much weight given to assessment *of* learning (summative assessment) and too little on assessment *for* learning (formative assessment) and assessment *as* learning (assessment focused on how to learn). In the examples, assessment *as* learning is mostly done implicitly and integrated into the learning activities. Therefore, our advice is to make self-regulation or metacognitive skills explicit to students by developing assessment *as* learning tasks and by formulating corresponding intended learning outcomes – for example, outcomes in which students reflect on team cooperation.

Powerful feedback

The well-considered use of feedback is a prerequisite for achieving meaningful assessment. We would emphasize that this is one of the most powerful ways to strengthen the learning process. In line with Hattie and Timperley (2007), our advice is that feedback (feed-up, feedback, and feed-forward) on the process and self-regulation level is most beneficial to the learning process of students when it comes to the higher-order learning outcomes that are a central part of this handbook. For more on the theory of powerful feedback, see page 18. This handbook provides some best practices of feedback at the self-regulation level. An example is *The evaluation of golden principles of collaboration* (example 8) where students formulate their own set of principles while working in a team, reflect on their collaboration, and at the end of the course receive feed-forward from each other on how to collaborate in future teams. We would also emphasize the importance of a safe class environment and the timing of feedback.

Alignment of assessment with the intended learning outcomes and assignments

Assessment is also more meaningful when you specify clearly and precisely what it is you want your students to learn and decide what you and your students take as evidence (the assessment criteria). That way, you can create assignments that allow students to develop and reflect on the intended knowledge or skills. To empower students, create opportunities and assessment forms for the students and yourself to assess where they are in achieving the intended learning outcomes. As stated in the introduction, alignment between learning outcomes, learning activities, and assessment is essential for creating a meaningful learning environment for students (Biggs, 2011). Courses are part of learning trajectories that add up to a certain level of knowledge, skills, and attitudes, and therefore alignment between courses in a program is essential. In this sense, developing and assessing higher-order skills requires alignment of the assessment at the program level in addition to more focus on the development of assessments of single courses.

Many learning outcomes of interdisciplinary courses are located higher up in Bloom's taxonomy. It can be more difficult to formulate concrete and measurable learning outcomes and the corresponding assessment criteria for these higher-order learning goals. A common mistake is to reduce the assessment to what can be easily and reliably marked. If you lose the alignment in your course, students will not learn exactly what you want them to learn, and assessment will become less meaningful. For example, the installation rubric (example 2), the crossing boundary rubric (example 3), and the rubric for interdisciplinary capstone projects (example 6) show how lecturers have translated learning outcomes into concrete assessment criteria.

Alignment of assessment with your pedagogical beliefs

One of the insights provided by the examples in the handbook is that assessment methods should also be aligned with how you teach. Your choice for an assessment method sends a certain message to students about your pedagogical beliefs. For example, when you are practicing a collegial pedagogy – which entails equal status for lecturers and students – it is best to choose an assessment method that gives students an equal role. In example 15, students were asked to develop and draw up their own learning outcomes and develop a grading rubric themselves. In this sense, the assessment method is aligned with the didactic principles of the course. Another example of an assessment method that is aligned with the didactical principles of the lecturers is the assessment where students are given ownership of their learning and a certain degree of leeway in how to realize the learning goals (example 7).

Making assessment more meaningful means revisiting what you mean by 'learning'. That is why it is important to reflect on your pedagogical beliefs and assumptions on learning (as well as those underlying the academic program). The next step is to develop corresponding assessment formats and make clear to students what is being asked of them. As Mieke Lopes Cardozo, one of the pioneers featured in this handbook (example 16), says: 'I want my students to develop as agents of change. I came to realize that this did not always take place. That is why I needed to step away from assessment forms that are very technical and standardized and to widen the view of what university education can bring.'

Authentic assessment tasks

There is not one single recipe for the meaningful assessment of interdisciplinary skills. Having said that, the examples in this handbook do highlight the effectiveness and wide use of one method in particular: authentic assessment tasks, which provide students with context by strongly resembling situations in which the assessed skills and knowledge are used in practice. These tasks are representative of the challenges that students will face in the world outside of the university and in their future professional life. Examples 4, 11, and 16 feature some best practices of authentic assessment. For instance, in example 16, students represent actors in a debate in which they apply the knowledge they obtained in the course *Education development and social justice*. In this way, the relevance of the obtained knowledge is very clear to the students, and the assessment is perceived as fun and engaging.

Taking the next steps

Whether you are teaching in an innovative interdisciplinary program or a more traditional course with a long tradition of summative assessment, you can break new ground and take steps to create a culture that emphasizes meaningful assessment to improve student learning. Below, we give recommendations on how to go about making a change.

Our first suggestion is to start small and develop and adjust your current practice towards more meaningful assessment over time. For example, when you introduce a new assessment method, allocate only 10% of the grade to this new method and keep the old one more or less in place. This gives you freedom to experiment and to evaluate and develop the method further for the next time. You could also start with some modifications of existing assessment protocols. So start small, evaluate, and adjust if necessary. Taking one step at a time is better than being overwhelmed and not starting at all. We advocate for an organic approach: an evolution rather than a revolution in assessment. This may sound modest, but in our view, it is a powerful way to achieve and sustain your goals.

Our second recommendation is to take some time to envision what your pedagogical beliefs and values are before you bring your new assessment strategy in practice. Some questions that can initiate and guide this reflection are: What are you trying to achieve in your students with your teaching? In ten years' time, what will students remember from this course? When you were a student, how were you taught and how has this influenced your teaching? By aligning your underlying beliefs with your assessment practice, you can make assessment more meaningful.

Our third recommendation is to collaborate and learn from like-minded colleagues within your program or institution. It takes a good deal of courage to transform your assessment practice from being test-oriented to being learning-oriented. As with most curriculum changes, changing the way you assess can generate heated debates. Search for and connect with colleagues to make sure you have sparring partners when developing assessment *for* and *as* learning, especially since assessment *for* and *as* learning are still rather new in academia compared with summative assessment. Interacting with others about how they overcame similar issues and structured their assessment can yield practical ideas and solutions. They can give you the support you need and inspire you to explore new ideas.

The need for interdisciplinary knowledge and skills continues to grow by the day. In this handbook, we have presented the best practices that demonstrate how these skills can be assessed with a purpose in mind. This book contributes to making meaningful assessment achievable. It takes time and requires a serious investment on your part, but it is definitely worthwhile. We have a responsibility to educate the next generation and are just at the beginning of a new era in which science and society are becoming more and more interconnected in order to tackle the complex challenges our societies face. The world is changing, education is changing, and assessment must be meaningful so that we can prepare our students for the future.

Index

The tables below give an overview of the examples that are elaborated in this handbook, arranged according to the skills for interdisciplinary understanding that you want to assess (table 1), the specific characteristics of the assessment (table 2), the roles of those involved (table 3), and the purpose of the assessment (table 4).

Table 1: Examples linked to skills assessed.

Example		integration	collaboration	critical thinking	reflection
1	Assessing perspective-taking skills with a simulation game	✓	✓	✓	
2	Making 'big ideas' tangible with an installation	✓		✓	✓
3	Self-assessment of boundary-crossing competences	✓	✓		✓
4	Peer feedback on the reflection of a stakeholder dialogue		✓		✓
5	Experiencing the learning process using a portfolio	✓			✓
6	A rubric for interdisciplinary capstone projects	✓	✓	✓	
7	Making failure a learning tool for collaboration skills		✓		✓
8	Evaluation of the golden principles of collaboration		✓		✓
9	Reflection on teamwork and disciplinary expert roles		✓		✓
10	A moot court to build critical thinking skills	✓		✓	
11	Authentic assessment, learning by accident	✓		✓	
12	Grading the contribution to class discussions	✓	✓	✓	
13	Dance assessment as experiential learning			✓	✓
14	Enhancing critical thinking with Perusall			✓	✓
15	Co-creation of a rubric to encourage ownership of learning				✓
16	Peer and self-assessment for student-led activities		✓		✓
17	From feed-up to feed forward				✓
18	Comparative judgment as a tool for learning		✓	✓	
19	The co-creation of assessment criteria		✓		
20	Reflection on interdisciplinary competences using a portfolio	✓	✓	✓	✓

Table 2: Examples linked to characteristics of assessment.

Example		authentic assessment	portfolio assessment	assessment with rubrics	group assessment	self-regulated learning
1	Assessing perspective-taking skills with a simulation game	✓		✓	✓	
2	Making 'big ideas' tangible with an installation			✓	✓	
3	Self-assessment of boundary-crossing competences					✓
4	Peer feedback on the reflection of a stakeholder dialogue	✓			✓	
5	Experiencing the learning process using a portfolio	✓				
6	A rubric for interdisciplinary capstone projects	✓				
7	Making failure a learning tool for collaboration skills			✓		✓
8	Evaluation of the golden principles of collaboration	✓			✓	✓
9	Reflection on teamwork and disciplinary expert roles	✓				
10	A moot court to build critical thinking skills	✓			✓	
11	Authentic assessment, learning by accident	✓			✓	
12	Grading the contribution to class discussions	✓				
13	Dance assessment as experiential learning			✓		
14	Enhancing critical thinking with Perusall					✓
15	Co-creation of a rubric to encourage ownership of learning	✓			✓	✓
16	Peer and self-assessment for student-led activities	✓			✓	✓
17	From feed-up to feed forward					✓
18	Comparative judgment as a tool for learning					✓
19	The co-creation of assessment criteria	✓				✓
20	Reflection on interdisciplinary competences using a portfolio		✓			✓

Table 3: Roles linked to the assessment examples.

Example		self-assessment	peer assessment	teacher-led assessment
1	Assessing perspective-taking skills with a simulation game		■	■
2	Making 'big ideas' tangible with an installation			■
3	Self-assessment of boundary-crossing competences	■		
4	Peer feedback on the reflection of a stakeholder dialogue	■	■	
5	Experiencing the learning process using a portfolio	■		
6	A rubric for interdisciplinary capstone projects			■
7	Making failure a learning tool for collaboration skills	■	■	
8	Evaluation of the golden principles of collaboration	■		
9	Reflection on teamwork and disciplinary expert roles	■		■
10	A moot court to build critical thinking skills		■	■
11	Authentic assessment, learning by accident	■		■
12	Grading the contribution to class discussions			■
13	Dance assessment as experiential learning		■	
14	Enhancing critical thinking with Perusall		■	
15	Co-creation of a rubric to encourage ownership of learning	■		■
16	Peer and self-assessment for student-led activities	■	■	
17	From feed-up to feed forward	■		■
18	Comparative judgment as a tool for learning		■	■
19	The co-creation of assessment criteria	■	■	■
20	Reflection on interdisciplinary competences using a portfolio	■		■

Table 4: Examples linked to purpose of assessment.

Example		of learning	for learning	as learning
1	Assessing perspective-taking skills with a simulation game		■	
2	Making 'big ideas' tangible with an installation		■	
3	Self-assessment of boundary-crossing competences			■
4	Peer feedback on the reflection of a stakeholder dialogue		■	
5	Experiencing the learning process using a portfolio		■	
6	A rubric for interdisciplinary capstone projects	■		
7	Making failure a learning tool for collaboration skills		■	
8	Evaluation of the golden principles of collaboration	■		
9	Reflection on teamwork and disciplinary expert roles	■		
10	A moot court to build critical thinking skills	■		
11	Authentic assessment, learning by accident	■		
12	Grading the contribution to class discussions	■		
13	Dance assessment as experiential learning	■		
14	Enhancing critical thinking with Perusall		■	
15	Co-creation of a rubric to encourage ownership of learning			■
16	Peer and self-assessment for student-led activities		■	
17	From feed-up to feed forward		■	
18	Comparative judgment as a tool for learning		■	
19	The co-creation of assessment criteria			■
20	Reflection on interdisciplinary competences using a portfolio			■

References

Allen, J.G., Fonagy, P., & Bateman, A.W. (2008). *Mentalizing in clinical practice*. American Psychiatric Pub.

Benda, L., Poff, N., Tague, C., Palmer, M., Pizzuto, H., Cooper, S., Stanley, E., & Modlen, G. (2002). How to avoid train wrecks when using science in environmental problem solving. *Bio-science 52*(12), 1127-1136.

Bergmann, M., Jahn, T., Knobloch, T., Krohn, W., Pohl, C., & Schramm, E. (2012). *Methods for transdisciplinary research: A primer for practice*. Campus Verlag.

Biggs, J.B. (2011). *Teaching for quality learning at university: What the student does*. McGraw Hill Education (UK).

Bloom, B.S. (1956). *Taxonomy of educational objectives: The classification of educational goals*. Longman.

Boix Mansilla, V.B. (2016). Interdisciplinary learning: A cognitive-epistemological foundation. *Oxford Handbook of Interdisciplinarity*, 2nd edition.

Boix Mansilla, V.B., & Duraising, E.D. (2007). Targeted assessment of students' interdisciplinary work: An empirically grounded framework proposed. *The Journal of Higher Education, 78*(2), 215-237.

Boix Mansilla, V.B, Miller, W.C., & Gardner, H. (2000). On disciplinary lenses and interdisciplinary work. In: P. Grossman, & S. Wieburg (eds.), *Interdisciplinary curriculum: challenges to implementation* (pp. 17-38). Teachers College Press.

Bransford, J.D., Brown, A.L., & Cocking, R.R. (2000). *How People Learn: Brain, Mind, Experience, and School*. National Academy Press.

Cannon-Bowers, J.A., & Salas, E. (1997). A framework for developing team performance measures in training. In: M.T. Brannick, E. Salas, & C. Prince (eds.), *Series in applied psychology. Team performance assessment and measurement: theory, methods and applications* (pp. 45-62). Lawrence Erlbaum Associates.

Cooke, N.J. & Hilton, M.L. (2015). *Enhancing the effectiveness of team science*. National Academies Press.

De Greef, L., Post, G., Vink C., & Wenting L. (2017). *Designing interdisciplinary education: a practical handbook for university teachers*. Amsterdam University Press.

Earl, L. & Katz, S. (2006). *Rethinking Classroom Assessment with Purpose in Mind. Assessment for learning, assessment as learning, assessment of learning*. Manitoba Education, citizenship and youth.

Eigenbrode, S.D., O'Rourke M., Wulfhorst, J.D., Althoff, D.M., Goldberg, C.S., Merrill, K., Morse, W., Nielsen-Pincus M., Stephens, J., Wienowiecki, L., & Bosque-Pérez, N.A. (2007). Employing philosophical dialogue in collaborative science. *BioScience, 57*(1), 55-64.

Facione, P. (2011). *Measured reasons and critical thinking*. The California Academic Press.

Fonagy, P., Gergely, G., & Jurist, E.L. (2004). *Affect regulation, mentalization and the development of the self*. Karnac books.

Glantz, M.H. & Orlovsky, N.S. (1986). Desertification: Anatomy of a complex environmental process. In: K.A. Dahlberg & J.W. Bennett (eds.), *Natural Resources and People: Conceptual issues in interdisciplinary Research*. Westview Press.

Gulikers, J.T., Bastiaens, T.J., & Kirschner, P.A. (2004). A five-dimensional framework for authentic assessment. *Educational technology research and development, 52*(3), 67.

Hattie, J., & Timperley, H. (2007). The power of feedback. *Review of Educational Research, 77*(1), 81-112.

Ivanitskaya, L., Clark, D., Montgomery, G., & Primeau, R. (2002). Interdisciplinary learning: Process and outcomes. *Innovative Higher Education, 27*(2), 95-111.

Keestra, M. (2017b). Introduction: Multi-Level Perspectives on Interdisciplinary Cognition and Team Collaboration-Challenges and Opportunities. *Issues in Interdisciplinary Studies, 35*, 113-120.

Keestra, M. (2021). *Introduction to interdisciplinary research; Theory and practice* (2nd ed.) [manuscript submitted for publication], Amsterdam University Press.

Klein, J., & Newell W. (1996). Advancing Interdisciplinary Studies. In J. Gaff & J. Ratcliff, (eds.), *Handbook of the Undergraduate Curriculum* (393-415). Jossey-Bass.

Klein, J. (2010). A taxonomy of interdisciplinarity. *The Oxford handbook of interdisciplinarity, 15*, 15-30.

McKinsey Global Institute (2017). *Jobs lost, jobs gained: Workforce transitions in a time of automation*. McKinsey & Company.

Menken, S., & Keestra, M. (2016). *An introduction to interdisciplinary research: theory and practice*. Amsterdam University Press.

Morse, W.C., Nielsen-Pincus, M., Force, J.E., & Wulfhorst, J.D. (2007). Bridges and barriers to developing and conducting interdisciplinary graduate-student team research. *Ecology and Society, 12*(2).

Nilson, L.B., & Stanny, C.J. (2014). Specifications Grading: Restoring Rigor, Motivating Students, and Saving Faculty Time (Reprint edition). Stylus Publishing.

Nosich, G.M. (2012). *Learning to think things through: A guide to critical thinking across the curriculum*. Pearsons.

OECD (2014). *Fostering and measuring skills. Improving cognitive and non-cognitive skills to promote lifetime success*. The Organisation for Economic Co-operation and Development.

O'Rourke, M., Crowley, S., Eigenbrode, S.D., & Wulfhorst, J.D. (eds.) (2014). *Enhancing communication & collaboration in interdisciplinary research*. Sage Publications.

Paul, R., & Elder, L. (2007). Critical thinking; The art of Socratic questioning. *Journal of Development Education, 31*(1), 36.

Pintrich, P.R. (1995). Understanding self-regulated learning. *New directions for teaching and learning, 1995*(63), 3-12.

Schön, D.A. (1987). *Educating the reflective practitioner*. Jossey-Bass.

Terenzini, P.T., & Pascarella, E.T. (1991). Twenty years of research on college students: Lessons for future research. *Research in Higher Education, 32*(1), 83-92.

Wernli, D., Darbellay, F., & Maes, K. (2016). *Interdisciplinarity and the 21st century research-intensive university*. LERU. https://www.leru.org/publications/interdisciplinarity-and-the-21st-century-research-intensive-university.

Wisniewski, B., Zierer, K., & Hattie, J. (2020). The power of feedback revisited: A meta-analysis of educational feedback research. *Frontiers in Psychology, 10*, 3087.

Colophon

About the authors

Ilja Boor is senior lecturer in psychobiology and an experienced educational innovator at the Teaching and Learning Center at the University of Amsterdam. The central theme of her education and innovations is self-regulated learning. As an educational innovator, she is specialized in the evidence-based conversion of didactic principles into educational innovations at the curriculum level and strengthening the collaboration of teacher teams.

Debby Gerritsen is a senior lecturer at the bachelor's program of Interdisciplinary Social Science and the interdisciplinary Research Master Social Sciences at the University of Amsterdam. She is specialized in developing interdisciplinary and transdisciplinary research projects for students in which she combines her expertise on research methods and interdisciplinary and transdisciplinary education.

Linda de Greef is program manager at the Institute for Interdisciplinary Studies at the University of Amsterdam. She is an experienced advisor and administrator within higher scientific education. She is specialized in interdisciplinary and transdisciplinary learning and teaching, vision and strategy development, innovation and development, and the professional development of interdisciplinary teaching skills.

Jessica Rodermans is program manager at the Institute for Interdisciplinary Studies at the University of Amsterdam. She develops and coordinates university-wide electives and honors courses with interdisciplinary topics in cooperation with lecturers from all faculties of the university. Within the field of educational sciences, her focus lies on feedback and interdisciplinary cooperation.

About the series

In previous publications, authors of the Institute of Interdisciplinary Studies have addressed several topics regarding interdisciplinary teaching and learning. Volume 3 of the Series Perspectives on Interdisciplinarity, *Designing Interdisciplinary Education*, offers accessible guidance and practical advice for university teachers and curriculum leaders who aim to develop, implement, and sustain a successful interdisciplinary approach to their teaching such as formulating interdisciplinary learning outcomes, embedding integration in the program design, and using didactic methods that nurture interdisciplinary understanding (De Greef, Post, Vink & Wenting, 2017). Volume 4 in the same series, *Interdisciplinary Learning Activities*, contains examples of learning activities that university teachers can use to teach and foster interdisciplinary skills in graduate and undergraduate students (Edelbroek, Mijnders & Post, 2018). This current handbook builds on these works and on the available literature about interdisciplinary education, assessment, authentic assessment, and the role of feedback in assessment. Additionally, it builds on our many years of experience improving assessment methods and using it creatively to influence students' learning.

About the University of Amsterdam

The University of Amsterdam (UvA) provides academic training in all areas of science and scholarship, and welcomes students and staff – from all backgrounds, cultures and faiths – who wish to devote their talents to the development and transfer of academic knowledge as a rich cultural resource and foundation for sustainable progress.

About the Institute for Interdisciplinary Studies

The Institute for Interdisciplinary Studies (IIS) is the UvA's knowledge centre for interdisciplinary learning and teaching. It develops new courses in collaboration with the faculties. The IIS has more than fifteen years' experience in interdisciplinary education and continuously develops substantive education innovations with an interdisciplinary character. The institute identifies new themes and issues linked to current developments in academia and society. Over 3,000 students study at the IIS. The IIS offers a number of interdisciplinary study programs along with a wide range of electives (minors, honors modules and various public events) for students from any faculty, staff and members of the public. All its activities are interdisciplinary in nature and are designed in collaboration with one or more faculties.

Contact

Institute for Interdisciplinary Studies
Science Park 904
1098 XH Amsterdam
Tel. +31 20 525 51 90
www.iis.uva.nl
E-mail: onderwijslab-iis@uva.nl

For Product Safety Concerns and Information please contact our EU
representative GPSR@taylorandfrancis.com
Taylor & Francis Verlag GmbH, Kaufingerstraße 24, 80331 München, Germany

www.ingramcontent.com/pod-product-compliance
Lightning Source LLC
Chambersburg PA
CBHW080412300426
44113CB00015B/2490